WALKING
THROUGH
HISTORY

WALKING THROUGH HISTORY

Anthony Burton

Macdonald
Queen Anne Press

A *Queen Anne Press* Book

© Anthony Burton 1988

First published in Great Britain in 1988 by
Queen Anne Press, a division of
Macdonald & Co (Publishers) Ltd
3rd Floor
Greater London House
Hampstead Road,
London NW1 7QX.

A BPCC plc Company.

British Library Cataloguing in Publication Data

Burton, Anthony
    Walking through history.
    1. Historic sites – Great Britain – Guide-Books. 2. Great Britain – Description and
    travel – 1971- – Guide-books
I. Title
914.1'04858   DA632

ISBN 0-356-15139-5

Produced for Queen Anne Press by
Curtis Garratt Limited
The Old Vicarage
Horton cum Studley
Oxford OX9 1BT

Maps by Taurus Graphics
Typeset by Dublin University Press Limited

Printed in Great Britain by
Butler & Tanner Ltd, Frome and London

CONTENTS

INTRODUCTION

The first thing that has to be said about walking into history is that we do so whenever we walk anywhere at all, whether we know it or not. History is there all around us, written on the land. Sometimes its message appears in banner headlines so large that no-one can avoid them: the rotted stump silhouette of the ruined castle on the hill, the skeletal tracery of the ancient abbey announce stories of power and piety. Elsewhere the writing might be more secretive, a straggling all-but-indecipherable script. A few faint marks may be all that remain to show where a medieval village once stood. But whether the message comes strong and clear or weak and coded, it is there all the time – all we have to do is to learn to recognise it. There are professionals, archaeologists, industrial archaeologists, and landscape historians, who spend their lives studying the landscape. They wish to solve the problems of the past, and turn to the landscape to help provide the answers. But there are others who take a quite different route. They come to the landscape for pleasure – and discover history.

I began walking for the simple pleasure of enjoying exercise, fresh air, and scenery just as thousands of others have done. When I was a schoolboy stomping over the hills of Yorkshire, there was a pride in covering so many miles a day, a sense of achievement in reaching a set number of peaks in the middle of a snowy winter. I certainly loved the scenery I met along the way, and there are certain images that I can still call to mind with total clarity: a straggle of drystone walls up a hillside, the purity of line of a snow cornice bowing to the void from the top of a high ridge. I cannot, however, recall thinking much about history. That was a subject for the classroom. It was Repeal of the Corn Laws and the tedium of memorizing dates. I was quite content to accept the scenery, without thinking too much about the role of humanity in shaping it. There was, in any case, little time to ponder such matters when there were always more miles to be tucked away before a final halt could be called to the day's exertions. Whether or not accumulating years bring any great increase in wisdom is open to doubt, but they do slow you down. Walking becomes less a matter of head down and bash on regardless: the pace becomes more leisurely, time can be set aside for stopping and looking. And, over the years, my view of the landscape has changed. It is no longer just a physical challenge, no longer even just a place of scenic beauty. It has become, quite simply, the best history book I could ever read.

This is not intended to be a text-book on the landscape, nor indeed a text-book on anything else but, instead, it aims to show how an awareness of history can add immensely to the enjoyment of walking. But why is it necessary to walk to enjoy the historical landscape? Is

A signpost to the past on Bignor Hill, Sussex.

walking any better than, say, driving to a site of historical interest, wandering about for a while and then getting in the car to go home again? The answer to that question depends on how you view history. To some, history consists of a series of great events, events which fundamentally change the course of human development: a battle replaces one dynasty with another, an Act of Parliament marks a decisive change in the organization of society, the old king dies and a new takes his place. These are the events recorded by the chroniclers of the time, but they are by no means the only events to affect the lives of the people. To a yeoman farmer, the arrival of a new kind of plough may be of far greater significance than a foreign war, and may well result in far more significant changes in the use of the land. Once you start to think of history as being the history of all the people, not just the mighty and influential, then the concept of an 'historic site' begins to lose its overwhelming importance. Obviously, there are sites where the atmosphere of the past is so strong that they achieve a special place in our understanding of their period. But, it is equally true that even the most important and spectacular sites gain in significance when they can be seen in the context of a broader canvas. It is the steady painting-in of the small details that helps to create the wider picture and those details only appear through careful observation. And that is not possible when you speed through the countryside on wheels.

There is another factor at work as well. History is not like one of the 'pure' sciences. There are no scales on which you can weigh and measure the past. It must be, to some extent, an act of imagination. Those who want to understand the life of the past must learn to think themselves into the circumstances of the past. It is only in very recent times that humans have been able to move rapidly all around the country. Until the arrival of the steam locomotive, the best that people could achieve by way of speed depended on having fast horses to ride. Even that luxury was reserved for the few: for the great majority of the citizens, to travel meant to walk. If you want to see the landscape as it was seen by the inhabitants of Tudor England, let alone see it as it was viewed a thousand years ago, then you must travel at the speed at which they travelled. You must walk.

Once you start walking and looking around you with the notion that the landscape we see today must, in some measure, have grown out of human activity, then you will find questions start to leap at you from all directions. What are those bumps on the land? Why does this road bend and twist? Why is this village where it is? Why is that house built in that particular way? There will be places where all signs of the past may seem to have been obliterated. A modern housing estate may have covered over an area of land and left nothing of the old on view. Yet even the least likely places may hold surprises. I remember visiting an estate on the edge of Leeds, on the boundary of which was a wall and in that wall were a number of stone blocks, each drilled with a hole. They were originally drilled to carry iron rails, and they represented almost the only physical remains of the Middleton Colliery Railway, the first commercial steam railway in the world. I would not pretend that there are similar discoveries to be made on many similar estates but it does, I think, show that even the unlikeliest settings may have secrets waiting to be discovered.

The aim of this book is a modest one, not to show historians how to find evidence of the past in the landscape, but to show how thinking about the past, being aware of the past, and, occasionally, going a little out of your way to find reminders of the past can add enormously to the pleasures of walking. The walks that follow were selected because each has a number of particularly interesting sites along the way, but most importantly of all, they are enjoyable as walks, pure and simple. What I hope to show is that the history simply makes them a great deal more pleasurable. Each walk is based on a specific historical period. Now, to a certain extent, this is a very artificial distinction. The country is never static: each generation brings its own changes to the land and nowhere, not even the most barren moor or the wildest heathland, has remained altogether untouched by people. So nowhere can be said to be an unspoilt, a purely medieval, or an industrial revolution landscape. The periods I have selected provide the dominant themes, but do not represent the whole story. There are, however, certain advantages in choosing a period as a main theme, if only because it provides a benchmark against which other changes can be measured. Why, looking at examples from two of the early walks, should the prehistoric trackway have been virtually ignored by later roadbuilders, while the Roman road is so often followed? Answering these questions supplies an insight into the ways in which each generation builds on the foundations laid down in an earlier age.

The periods chosen are not exactly evenly spaced, but change does not occur at a smooth, even rate. If one takes a walk with 'prehistoric' theme, what exactly does the word mean? If we take 'history' as implying written records, then the first appearance of the name 'Pritani' which was later to become 'Britain' takes us back no further than the Celts of the fourth century BC. Back beyond that stretches the Bronze Age and the Stone Ages, and a time around half a million years ago when the first people appeared in Britain. Given that sort of timescale, it seems less than fair to devote just one walk to the theme of prehistory. Yet this was

a period, when in comparison with our own times, change moved almost infinitesimally slowly, and it is this which makes it sensible to devote just one-eighth of the book to cover more than nine-tenths of the period covered by the whole.

The walks themselves vary considerably in length, and that length has been determined partly by the nature of the historical remains and partly because I wanted each walk to have a sense of completeness. I am not suggesting that the reader should set off and follow in my footsteps: what I hope to show is how to plan a historical walk for yourself and how to recognize and appreciate what you see along the way. For those who do fancy taking the same routes, I should give a brief word of caution. Firstly, please remember that you will have to do as I did and keep to established footpaths or to common land. All the walks require that you

One of the many small bridges and culverts on the old road. In the distance, dwarfed by the mountains of Glencoe, is the tiny croft, Blackrock Cottage.

arrive properly equipped, and that means walking boots, weatherproof clothing, maps, and compass – all the equipment, in fact, that an experienced walker would expect to take on a long and occasionally quite arduous trek. This is not the place for a lecture on walking equipment, but there is one basic rule: always err on the side of caution. I do not want to give the impression that these walks are some kind of hazardous assault course, an Outward Bound for historians. They are not. And there is one other point to bear in mind in planning a walk of this type: allow plenty of time. These walks need to be leisurely, for you need time to pause and look. If in doubt as to whether to take two days or three, opt for three. In the end, I hope that the walks will give as much pleasure to the reader as they did to me – and I hope too that they will inspire an urge to find history walks of your own.

THE ANCIENT TRACK

Eastbourne to Buriton, 75 miles (120 km). OS maps 197, 198, 199.

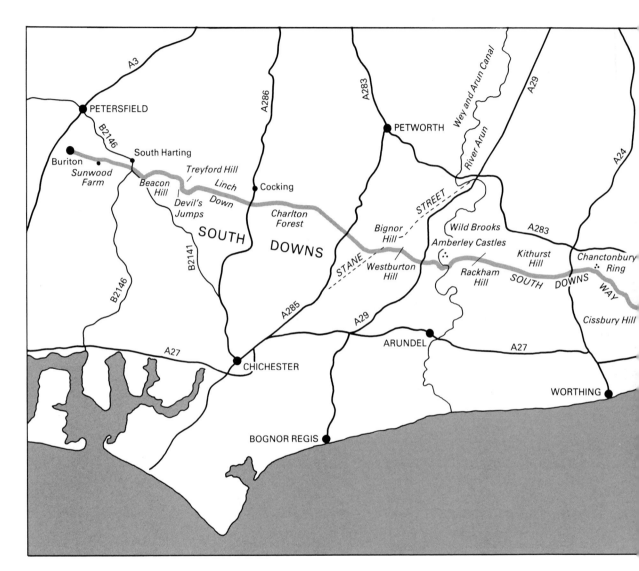

This is a walk along one of the officially designated long-distance footpaths of Britain, the South Downs Way. I have called this an ancient track because tradition has it that it was used as a major transport route in distant, prehistoric times – and tradition is by no means to be despised, even if it is not always backed up by hard, scientifically attested evidence. But to describe a way as ancient is to raise a whole number of questions – how ancient, what do we mean by 'trackway' and, most importantly, how do we know that the answers to the first two

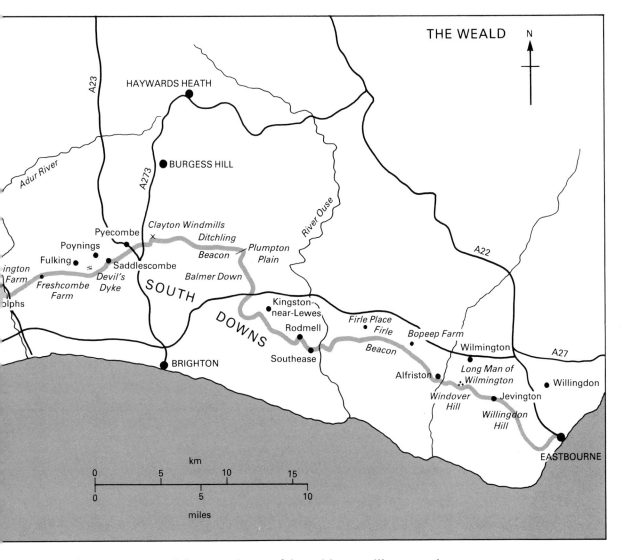

questions are accurate? Some, at least, of the evidence will appear along
the walk, but first we have to remind ourselves that when we look out
across the scenery, we are looking not at one history, but two. There is
the familiar story of human history and the other history, covering the
almost unimaginable ages of geological time. There can be no complete
understanding of the former unless we take some account of the latter.
One advantage of the South Downs walk is that the area is one of
comparatively simple patterns.

The South Downs Way

For our purposes, the story begins after the first rocks were laid down, at the time when a vast, freshwater lake covered the whole region. Sands and clays formed on the lake bed, but the sea broke through to swamp almost the whole landmass and drown out the lake. In this period, the sea was rich with shellfish, including microscopic organisms, known as Foraminifera, as well as equally tiny, single-celled algae protected by chalky plates called coccoliths. As the animals and plants died and sank to the bottom, they rotted, leaving only their hard shells behind. The Foraminifera account for about a tenth of the soft, white rock we know as chalk; the rest is composed of coccoliths and the small shells of a vast variety of other sea creatures. Among these were sponges, whose skeletons would, in time, go towards the formation of the very hard flint which can be found as nodules embedded in the chalk. The sea at last receded, leaving a land where chalk overlay the sands and clays. Then came a period of upheaval, when the earth buckled and twisted to throw up mountains and hills, including a vast dome that stretched in an unbroken line from southern England across into France. Wind and water ate their way through the dome: the sea broke through to separate England from France, and the central part of the dome was steadily eroded. This is the landscape we see today: the chalk hills of the North and South Downs surround a valley where the chalk has been eroded to expose the soft sands and clays of the Weald, while to the south lies the narrow strip of the coastal plain. This may all sound a very long way from conventional notions of history, but it represents no more than the briefest of brief sketches of events covering many millions of years. These were the natural forces which created the land with which people had somehow to come to terms.

Man's first appearance came a mere half-million years ago, when Britain was still part of continental Europe, but we shall see few signs of that distant past along our downland walk. So we need to start thinking about a time some 5000 years ago, the Neolithic or New Stone Age. When we talk of the South Downs Way as an ancient trackway, we are saying in effect that this was a recognized, regularly travelled route at this time. We can start to find out what it all means, once we set out on the walk.

The beginning certainly offered few incentives to think about neolithic man, for I set out from Eastbourne railway station for a trudge through the suburbs to the start of the walk proper on Paradise Down. It seemed far from paradisal on that particular afternoon in May, for the rain teemed down, the sort of fine yet persistent rain that seems to find its way into every crevice of even the best protective clothing. This is perhaps an appropriate place to make a few points about this particular walk. Firstly, it is a long one which offers little in the way of shelter, so you need to be provided with clothing that will keep off the worst of the weather, either the torrential rain that I was experiencing or a fierce sun. Secondly, because of the nature of the walk along the high ridge, you need to come off the downs if you want someone else to feed and house you. Stopping places are few and if, like me, you prefer a bed under a roof to a sleeping bag in a tent, then you will have to book in advance. And you will find days when it is easier to carry your own food and drink rather than make a long detour – and it is in any case a good idea to take your own supply of drinking water, for you will rarely find any along the way. Lack of water was not, however, my immediate problem as I turned off the metalled road on to the bridleway marked by a South Downs plinth. All along the way the path is clearly marked by plinths and signposts.

At first, this is little more than a rough track over grassland spotted by bushes and scrub with woodland on the side, the latter containing what at first glance appears to be a flying saucer that has recently landed, but is nothing more glamorous than a covered-in reservoir. The guide books will all tell you of the superb views from this part of the walk, but I have nothing to record but driving rain that shot out of the misty greyness that covered the hillside. The white chalk of the pathway was turned to a dull, grey slither as I climbed to the main road and crossed on to the golf course. If there was not much in the shape of distant views, then at least there was time to muse on matters nearer to hand, such as the strange behaviour of the human species that goes out in such atrocious weather for fun. For I was not alone. Ahead of me, the golfers played on, undeterred. Other thoughts, rather more pertinent to the history of the landscape, came to mind. Along the way I should be seeing features on the ground which would suggest ways in which early man lived – symmetrical marks cut into the ground, artificial mounds raised on high. What I wondered would an archaeologist of the distant future make of a golf course, assuming all written records had been destroyed? A complex of eighteen levelled patches, joined by distinct tracks, each track surrounded by raised earthworks: that might suggest some strange ritual or a settlement of huts, with holes for central supporting posts. Would anyone deduce the game of golf from the evidence? It is as well to remember that we too might be making some quite wrong deductions from the marks left behind thousands of years ago.

Underfoot, the chalk glistened damply through the grass, wet certainly, but the hard flint showed through and where, in clayey soil, the going would have been reduced to a muddy wallow, here it remained reasonably firm. Bearing in mind the nature of the Weald to the north, with its sand and clays, the advantage of an upland route in an age before surfaced roads were constructed, became obvious. The track across the Downs is a good, firm way, but to say that it is a good way is not to say that it was, in fact, in use. I had not yet seen any evidence that early man ever came this way at all.

Willingdon Hill was in cloud but, as I crossed the summit, the cloud suddenly began to tear and separate and, for the first time, the true downland scene opened out like a spectacular theatre set revealed by the rising curtain. This grand opening was celebrated by a fanfare of birdsong, dominated by the high treble of the lark. It was a sound that was never to be far away throughout the walk, though other less mellifluous characters occasionally joined the chorus, from the hollow hooting of the cuckoo to the harsh rattle of the partridge. The scene now revealed showed many of the features that characterize this landscape. This is ground that dips and sways, making gentle curves like a sheet held out to the wind. And these natural shapes have been accentuated by man, as fences follow the contours and the marks of the plough trace out the curves of the hills. The basic forms may be ancient, the result of age-long weathering, but the imposed pattern is essentially modern, for it is only in recent times that the high downland has been put to the plough.

The huge and mysterious figure of the Long Man of Wilmington carved into the hillside. Theories abound as to whether this is a depiction of a Saxon warrior, a Roman centurion, or some figure with mystical significance.

Even now, one can see what a poor soil this is for crops, with the white chalk everywhere showing through the pale green of shoots, and nodules of flint lying like models for Henry Moore sculptures on the ground. Something of an older pattern does still survive in the rough grassland dotted with grazing sheep, but the main impression is of wild country tamed, turned to arable land by the new techniques of machine-age farming. These new methods have largely obliterated traces of the more distant past – largely, but not entirely.

As I came down over the brow of the hill, I passed what appeared to be ancient stones, perhaps survivors from an old monastery or castle, but which are, in fact, nothing more romantic than the remains of Barclays Bank, Eastbourne set up here to create a picturesque effect.

But across the other side of the deep valley is a genuine survivor from the past, marked on the map as 'field system'. What I could see now was a pattern of small fields, clearly defined by earth banks round all four sides. The banks are known as lynchets and are typical of a prehistoric system which produced what we call Celtic fields, indicating that they were formed before the Roman conquest. They were too far away for detailed examination, but I should be seeing more of them along the way.

The path now disappeared into a sunken lane that led down to the valley of Jevington. The waters that collect in the Weald need an escape route, and rivers have carved their paths through the chalk hills. Sometimes, as here, the rivers have dried up, but always these gaps have provided a route by which people can move between the coast and the interior, and, where the gap appears, there the settlement grows. The most prominent feature, as in so many villages, is the church which itself provides a commentary on the changing history of the area. The most obvious feature is the huge, square tower, a vast structure for such a small, isolated community. It was built in the early tenth century, when the Saxon settlers were being raided from the nearby coast, and it may be that the massive tower was intended to provide a refuge and a defence against the invaders. Its story, however, goes back even further in time for, on the north and south faces, you can still see traces of early windows, their arched headings built from Roman bricks. Inside, there is another survivor from the Saxon period, a crudely carved yet sinuous Christ, somewhat absentmindedly impaling a demonic beast with a sword. The church interior has sections dating from many different periods, culminating in a fine Tudor roof and some less happy Victorian 'restorations'. The nineteenth century was a miserable age for country churches which all too often were to lose their basic simplicity and cohesion beneath a wealth of pseudo-medieval details and unfortunate stained glass. Jevington has escaped the worst, and on every hand there are reminders of the closeness of the sea: a ship's bell hangs in the tower, an anchor cross stands above the porch, and a splendid ship memorial can be seen in the churchyard. It is probably fair to say that it is all-but-impossible to walk round any old country church without finding something that will both please the eye and have a story to tell of the life of the area.

As I walked up the hill beyond the church, I soon realized that the outward show of wealth was all concentrated in the river valleys and in the rich land at the foot of the scarp face. Racehorses browsed in a field, while Jevington Place presented an urbane face to the world, an old house given a Georgian facelift to keep it in fashion. Once clear of the trees, however, and back on the open downland, ancient history made itself into a powerful presence. This is a convoluted landscape of twisting ridges and steep slopes, and the horizon was marked by low mounds, shown on the map as tumuli. These circular, obviously artificial hillocks are round barrows, marking the spot where Bronze Age people buried their dead some 3000 years ago. Many of the examples I met on this walk had hollow centres, the scars left by treasure hunters. In fact, little can be expected but bones and the shattered remnants of urns that once held the ashes of cremation. The one thing that such barrows do tell us is that there were settlements near here at one time, and their presence has been taken as corroborative evidence for the nature of the ancient trackway. Sadly, the evidence does not hold up. It was always possible that the high ridge was selected as a burial ground remote from the settlement, but, more importantly, we now know that there were other ancient burial sites down in the valleys – undiscovered for years because all traces had apparently been removed by ploughing.

Barrows crop up throughout the walk, but here on Windover Hill is one of the most spectacular and intriguing survivors from ancient times. If you look down the hillside, north towards Wilmington at a point above a prominent white chalk pit, you catch a glimpse of odd, white lines cut into the turf. Slowly, as you walk along, they begin to resolve into recognizable shapes; first feet, then a body, and finally the whole image can be seen, the outline of a man, arms outstretched carrying two long wands or spears. This is the famous Long Man of Wilmington. He stands over 60 metres (200 feet) tall, and seems strangely foreshortened until seen from a distant viewpoint in the valley, when the proportions all appear perfect. How old is the figure? He is certainly well over 1000 years old, and his stance is not unlike that of Roman soldiers seen on coins, holding standards in their hands. Then again, a belt buckle found locally showed a Saxon warrior with a pair of staves. Such similarities, however, are no help in explaining why such a huge figure was cut into the hill, surely too great an effort for a simple exercise in pictorial realism. It is hard not to see the Man as having some form of symbolic or ritual significance, and the whole figure is enclosed in a rectangle with a precise 2:1 ratio of the sides. Perhaps the best thing to do is to accept the official version – origin unknown – and enjoy the pleasures of speculation.

The Long Man is not the only ancient site on this hill, for if you walk on towards Alfriston and look back, you can see another mound outlined on the horizon, a mound, not round this time but flattened. Like the round barrow, the long barrow is a burial site, but here as many as fifty bodies could be interred, and this apparently insignificant interruption to the wide horizon represents one of the earliest examples of ancient monument known in Britain, for the long barrow dates right back to Neolithic times. This one hill had shown me remnants of a past that we know to date back thousands of years and one mysterious figure of uncertain age and even less certain significance. The path, however, was now leading me down to the valley and inevitably closer to our own time.

Once again I was approaching a valley, a north-south transport route through the gap and a settlement. Such settlements may not be large by modern standards, and often cannot be large because of the restricted space available, but they do frequently carry signs of former importance. Alfriston is a fine example, and a fine example, too, of the way in which the use of local materials adds so much to the visual pleasures we all get from old country towns and villages. As I came down to the valley of the gently wandering Cuckmere, the first prominent feature to catch the eye was inevitably the church. It stands in an unusual churchyard, circular and slightly raised, which is actually a prehistoric structure. It was by no means unusual for early church builders to adapt sites which were of pagan significance, hoping that the followers of the old religion would rapidly adapt to the new. It is known as the Cathedral of the Downs, which is perhaps a touch exaggerated, but it is an interesting building on a cruciform plan. It is worth pausing to consider the materials used for construction. The walk had already shown what was on offer on the downs: chalk, not a good building material even at its best; flint nodules, which at first glance seem little better; clay down in the valley; and timber. Church architects have always tried to use the very finest materials to emphasize the importance of the building but, without going to the immense expense of importing good-quality stone, what was to be done here? Until the present century, brick from the local clay was considered far too mundane for a church, so the only obvious candidate left is flint.

Flint possesses a very important property – it can be knapped, that is, if struck in the right way, flakes can be split from it. This was the technique used in Neolithic times to make tools and weapons, a subject we shall be coming back to later. Builders also found that the flints could be split to present a smooth, flat, shiny black face. Flints, however, are seldom very large so they have to be bound together by strong mortar to make a sound wall. Knapped flint walls of the type you can see on Alfriston church are the result of skilled craftsmanship and the effect is undeniably striking. Rising above the roof is the spire, and here the other widely available material comes into play, for it is built up of

The fifteenth-century Star Inn at Alfriston with its strange array of emblems. It also shows a remarkable range of building materials. The front elevation reveals a typical timber-framed building topped by a tiled roof, but the side reveals a flint wall with brick courses, while the upper wall is hung with tiles.

shingles, which could be described as small, wooden tiles. Timber features again in the fourteenth-century Clergy House next to the church, where the main structure is based on a wooden frame, topped by a thatched roof. It is a building of some historical interest, for at the end of the last century, it was in a sorry state of dilapidation and for many years the vicar of Alfriston fought a lonely battle for its preservation. Then, in 1896, he turned to a newly formed body, the National Trust, who agreed to purchase and restore it. It was to be their very first property.

Turning into the village itself, I found a street full of buildings presenting a whole series of variations on the theme of local materials: timber used for house frames and weather boarding; walls hung with rich, red tiles; curved pantiles forming sinuous patterns on roofs; and still more flint, sometimes knapped, sometimes used as rounded stones embedded in mortar. There is a small market place with a market cross, but by far the most impressive buildings are the inns: the fine, old, timber-framed George where I was to rest my feet and start to dry out somewhat sodden clothing, and the fifteenth-century Star Inn, with its exotic frontage. The Star began life as a hostelry for pilgrims but, in its later days as an inn, it acquired some colourful characters on the facade: Saint Michael spearing a basilisk, a gentleman who for some unaccountable reason appears to be trying to chew a length of rope and a ferocious red lion which, in the seventeenth century graced a Dutch

One of the few dew ponds still in use on the Downs — with survivors of the great flocks that once grazed the uplands.

warship. The inn also acquired some colourful characters on the inside. The sea is little more than 3 miles (5 km) away, and the old pilgrims' hostelry had slipped so far from grace as to become a favourite haunt of the local smugglers.

The next morning I set off along the lane that runs up past the Star's guardian lion and through the modern additions to Alfriston. The road is steep but, in the age of the motor car, this is no great deterrent to builders, and houses have spread upwards and outwards, away from the old valley road. The steep road gives way to a steeper path which offers superb views all along the way, with side valleys twisting and turning off to the south, while the scarp drops sharply away to the north. The map promises rich historical pickings, with long barrows, round barrows, and cross dykes all marked along the route but, in practice, they turn out to be disappointingly indistinct traces. Most of the barrows have been robbed out, and now they are no more than faint ripples on the long waving line of the horizon.

There are other features which, at first glance, might be mistaken for hollow, plundered barrows. Again there is a hollow, surrounded by raised earth, but here the hollow dips down below the general level of the land, so that the bank is no more than the earth removed when the hole was dug. These are dew ponds, dug to collect water, probably from the prevalent sea mists rather than actual dew, to serve the downland sheep. Most have now dried up, and no-one is quite certain how old they are, though the best guess is that they date back to some time in the eighteenth century.

The cross dykes are very easy to miss, for they now only appear as quite indistinct marks, the merest suggestion of a low ridge and a shallow ditch. Their function is equally unclear. It has been suggested that the ditches are hollow ways, paths worn down by centuries of use, but it seems more likely that they were once boundary markers.

I climbed on up past oddly named Bopeep Farm to the summit of Firle Beacon. To the north, I looked down on the villages strung out along the foot of the hill and an ornamental tower that marks the position of the parkland surrounding the grand house of Firle Place. To the south was the sea, but it was a misty blue that ran seamlessly into a faded, washed-out sky. Only the silhouettes of the dock cranes at Newhaven confirmed that there really was an edge to the land. Now my path lay downhill again, into the valley of the Ouse and into another very different landscape. The River Ouse has carved out a wide, flat plain on which I could see glittering, straight lines – too straight to be natural waterways. Once, this broad valley was a swampy wasteland, but drainage channels were cut to dry it out and bring it into use. This, however, is a fairly recent phenomenon in terms of the long history of the downs. In 1791, an Act of Parliament allowed for improvement of navigation on the river and 'the better Draining of the low lands'. There was a battle for many years over who should pay for the work – the

A typical downland scene. In the foreground, the South Downs Way is a broad, grassy track, with just a few traces of flint, but, in the distance, it appears as a distinct line of white chalk.

landowners who benefited from drainage or the river users who got better transport. As I got nearer to the valley floor, I began to see how all this had affected development – though there were distractions in the form of noisy bleepings from reversing trucks in the nearby chalk quarry.

The flat wetland seemed all but deserted, with the road clinging to the edge of the downland slope, and only the long, snaking track of the railway keeping the river company. One farm stands at the edge of the drained land, and a fine, prosperous place it looks too, with its walls of flint and hung tiles, and an extensive kitchen garden behind it. Its appearance is very distinctly Georgian, suggesting that someone at least did well out of the newly drained land. The road across the river is not useable by motor traffic, and the river itself is crossed by a swing bridge, a relic of the days when vessels came up and down the river under sail. Then the land begins to rise up out of this flood plain, and at once I was back with a far older settlement, the hamlet of Southease. It is a delightful spot, where the first church was founded more than 1000 years ago. The most obvious feature, however, is a comparative newcomer, the round tower having been added to the simple Saxon

The simple Saxon church at Southease, to which the distinctive round tower was added in the twelfth century.

church in the twelfth century. It stands by a village green, around which are grouped seventeenth-century thatched cottages, combining to make the sort of scene that is thought of as typically English, but is in reality quite rare. The most interesting feature of Southease, however, is to be found inside the church, a set of faded but still recognizable wall paintings, mostly dating from the middle of the thirteenth century. We tend to look at these tiny village churches and praise their essential simplicity, exclaiming over the plain carpentry of the wooden roof, but here is a reminder that many were once highly decorated, positively gaudy.

The road led on now to neighbouring Rodmell. Here the church is altogether grander but restorations have not been kind, for the interior is dominated by a modern imitation Norman arch which quite overwhelms everything else in sight. It is not actually on the line of the walk, but it has a lovely setting, and Bloomsburyites might care to make the diversion because, along the way, they will pass the former home of Leonard and Virginia Woolf. It was perhaps appropriate to musings over twentieth-century literature that it was just here that I met a solitary runner, bawling out curses and shouting damnation to the world at large.

The path out of Rodmell gives, as is true of so much of the way, some fine, wide vistas, but is itself a touch disappointing. Modern farming methods have covered almost the whole downland area with crops, leaving the walkway as a narrow corridor, here concreted for much of the way. But, as the path swung in a great arc around Cold Coombes, so the concrete came to an end and the views more than compensated for the earlier dullness. From here, it was possible to see how modern developments have taken a very different direction from those of the older villages I had seen along the way. Kingston-near-Lewes was once a village, but has grown in recent years by the addition of streets on a strictly formal grid, which takes no account of the shapes and patterns of the land. This is not, in fact, a new phenomenon – more a sign that growth has occurred over a short period of time according to an official plan. The medieval village was almost like an organic creation, changing and adapting over the years; but planners everywhere, whether ancient Romans or modern Britains, seem always to look for neat symmetry and a definable pattern. A symmetry of a different kind appeared in the splendid horseshoe bowl of the coombe, where the path turned back on itself to pass Newmarket plantation, a fine stand of timber dominated by the trees which epitomize this part of the country, the beech. After that it came as something of a shock to the system to find myself confronted by a dual carriageway with four lanes of fast cars to negotiate. I made a quick scamper across, just in time to catch a bus into Lewes for the night's rest, with the thought that I should have the same hazard to face again in the morning. I did not know that the traffic was to prove a comparatively minor obstacle to progress.

The morning main-road dash was uneventful. I climbed up out of the main-road cutting, and soon the angry hum of traffic was no more disturbing than the buzzing of a fly. I then entered a deep hollow way through a wood so dense and with a floor so deeply carpeted with ivy that the last vestiges of sound were cushioned and absorbed. That behind me, I crossed a stile into a field full of cattle and followed the well-trodden way towards another stile in the hedge opposite. It was only as I got closer to a group of cows that I became aware that one was of the opposite sex, heavy shouldered and boasting a wide spread of horns. The bull and I eyed each other. There is an often-repeated theory that a bull in the company of cows is a placid beast. That may well be, but my pace was getting notably quicker and the edge of the field seemed a long way off. It all passed without any problems, but my pulse rate when I left that field was several points higher than it had been when I entered.

I was now set on a straight, steady climb through huge fields tinted by the pale green of new growths that stood out against the white flecked, chalky soil. But then, as I climbed up Balmer Down towards a line of pylons, a different pattern appeared in the fields. Where modern farmers have marked out their land with wire fences, here I could see the remnants of a grid of earthen banks, topped by shrubs and bushes. It was far from complete, for ploughing had driven wide gaps through the banks, but enough remained to show that it represented the outline of a system of small, oblong fields laid out on the hillside. As these field boundaries were some distance away, it was not possible even to hazard a guess as to their age, but the field size, which can be confirmed from the 1:25 000 scale map shows them to be too small for any field system brought in over the past two centuries. And, with no village nearby, they seem unlikely to be part of any medieval common field. So we appear to be looking at a field system that probably dates back at least as far as the Roman occupation. It is another small fragment of evidence to confirm that early man did indeed settle up here on the downs, and if that was so, then he would certainly have found the ridge an ideal route to follow. Confirmation of an early settlement has been found in excavations just south of the way at Plumpton Plain.

The route now turned briefly north, then westward again to follow a line along the edge of the escarpment. This seemed as good a place as any to pause and take stock of the landscape. To the south, the sea remained as a distant prospect which often seemed indistinguishable from the sky: only the sharpness of the drop distinguishing a sea cliff from a downland scarp. In the distance, the towers of Brighton seemed more like the towers of some Disneyesque castle than office blocks and flats, while the tall chimneys of Portslade power station seemed to remain in sight for many miles. Turning the other way, the wide expanses of the Weald stretched away to the distant hills of the North Downs. It is still possible, viewing the whole area, to get a glimpse of how it must have been many centuries ago, for it is a region still dotted by woodland, and it is easy to see how the scattered fragments once joined in a blanket of trees. It is tempting to see a neat, historical pattern emerging. Up here on the hill, all man would need to do would be to scrape with primitive tools at the light soil to grow his crops, while the rough grassland would provide ample grazing for his animals. Down there, the heavy, waterlogged soil would never have yielded to such crude methods and the impenetrable forests and cloying clay would have combined to drive him to the uplands. The ample evidence of ancient fields and tumuli on the downs and their absence from the Weald might seem to support this view, but it is not that simple. Modern botanical research suggests that the downs, too, were once forested, though not as densely as the Weald; and the absence of ancient remains on the low ground is scarcely surprising given the intensive cultivation of modern times – cultivation on a scale which has only just begun to appear on the uplands. Nevertheless, as early as Neolithic times, people had the means to clear the downs of this probably skimpy covering. The name 'stone axe' probably suggests some kind of crude, cartoon-comedy object. But just pick up a flint fragment and feel the hardness and the sharpness of its edge. Properly fashioned, the polished flint axe was a very useable tool. Neolithic man certainly had the ability to hack his way through the downland trees and clear the ground with fire. How far he penetrated into the lower lands is largely speculative.

What is not in dispute is that the Weald was a hard land for people to conquer. Travel through its heavy clays was difficult and the forest was dense with massive trees. Yet you can see how patches have been carved out, to be filled with fields which are quite tiny in comparison with the wide hectares of modern factory farming. The impression is not so much of a country studded with woods as of enclaves in a continuous forest. Other patterns also appear. The land at the bottom of the scarp is liberally dotted with villages and settlements, taking advantage of the natural springs that appear through the chalk. Individual details stand out. You can easily pick out the rather grand, formal buildings of the agricultural college. A 'V' of trees on the hillside was planted to celebrate

Victoria's jubilee. Originally, they were intended to spell 'VR' but cash failed to match ambition.

Walking on across Ditchling Beacon, I came across one of the few farms actually built on the top of the ridge, but well sheltered from the prevailing winds by a horseshoe of trees. Ditchling Beacon itself is a popular spot, easily reached by road, with a concrete plinth, a triangulation point used in surveying, and a plaque pointing out places of interest, the latter long since vandalized. Even on this cold May day, a few motorists were there but they stayed, probably wisely, in their cars. From here, the way goes more-or-less due west towards Pyecombe, but I took a small diversion to the south to visit the Clayton windmills. We now think of windmills as quaint survivors from a byegone age, but they were once a vital part of rural life and are really quite modern. All manner of devices have been used to crush grain to make flour or meal. The oldest methods used stones worked by hand. The simplest form was the saddle quern, in which the grain was rubbed between two shaped stones, but sophistication arrived with the rotary quern where the lower stone was fixed and the upper stone turned round by a handle. It must soon have been apparent that if you made the stones big enough, they could be rotated by harnessing an animal to walk round a circular track. But, by the time Domesday Book came to be written, the water mill had become the principal means of grinding grain. A few centuries later, the windmill appeared.

My first sight of the mills was of a set of white sails poking over the brow of the hill, but it was only when I was practically on top of them that I realized that the two mills were of quite different types. Historically, one should start with the lower of the two mills, 'Jill' – traditionally, mills are female like ships, but this has not prevented the name 'Jack' being applied to the neighbour. Jill is a plain affair of white weatherboarding providing a cover for the machinery, turned through simple gearing by the sails. A mill, however, will only work when turned into the wind and this mill balances on a central post upon which it can pivot. It is a type known, in fact, as a post mill. In the simplest version, the whole of the body, the buck, was swung bodily round into the wind but this mill is a little more sophisticated. A fan tail is attached to the buck. When the mill is correctly positioned it is sheltered from the wind and cannot turn, but if the wind shifts it will rotate and act like a propeller to drive the buck round until it is again in the correct position. Jack is a later development. Millwrights came to realize that there was no need to move the entire buck, if you put sails and a fantail on a rotating cap at the top of a substantial mill. This is the system employed on the tower mill, Jack.

The post mill 'Jill'. The weather-boarded body or 'buck' carries the sails, which can be moved into position for setting by the pulley. The vane or fan-tail keeps the sails pointing up to the wind when the mill is working.

It is possible to keep straight on down the hill to the main road and rejoin the walk at Pyecombe, but the road is busy and has no footpath so it is rather more pleasant to retrace your steps and follow the path down by the golf course. Pyecombe has a simple, square-towered church and, opposite it, is a house with a large, single-storey extension which was once a forge supplying, among other things, shepherds' crooks. The iron end of a crook still forms the latch to the church gate. The route now goes past, or via, in my case, the Plough Inn, and inevitably having come downhill, I had then to climb back up again, if only for a short way for I was soon descending again to Saddlescombe. There is not much to the place, but from the hill above it you can tell that it has seen changes. The lines of an old road system are quite distinct, and the original coach road did, in fact, run at a higher level than the modern road, and there is a clear way down to the village centre. The surrounding fields display a regular pattern of bumps and hollows, suggesting that there might have been more buildings here at one time.

The farm in the valley bottom is a typically well-sited place, snuggling comfortably into a sheltering fold and surrounded by flint-walled barns, kitchen garden and duck pond – a self-contained, self-sufficient unit.

The path crosses the main road and follows a somewhat ill-defined route through scrubland bordering a minor road which, sadly, has made this a convenient spot for dumping old mattresses, car seats, and plastic bags that ooze rubbish. It was a little dispiriting, but then the scrub came to an end and I found myself faced by the most stunning scene to be found anywhere on the South Downs Way – the Devil's Dyke. The name 'dyke' generally suggests an artificial work but this is a natural phenomenon, a deep valley with precipitous sides carving out a great V-shaped notch in the face of the downs. Natural it may be, but it makes a truly formidable defensive barrier for anyone settled on top of the hill and, much as you would expect, there are clear signs of shallow ditches and ridges on the steep slopes of the dyke. There are rather more obvious signs of defence works when you reach the head of the valley. A road leads off towards the hotel in the centre of the plateau and, at a point marked by a group of trees, I found extensive earthworks which stretch across the narrow neck of land that separates the dyke from the steep escarpment that falls away towards Fulking. The whole plateau was thus defended and there is evidence of occupation at various periods from the Bronze Age onwards, but whether it was a permanent fort, a place to retreat to when danger threatened, or a defended settlement is uncertain. History, however, does not end with ancient man.

The Devil's Dyke had become a popular tourist attraction by the end of the eighteenth century and there has been a hotel up here since 1817. In 1879, the landlord decided to boost his tourist trade by bringing the Devil's Dyke into the modern world. So he built a 'Steep Grade Railway' up from Poynings. It worked on the balance principle, the weight of a descending train balancing that of the one going up the hill. And to add to the fun, there was a cable car ride across the gorge. The track of the railway can still be seen, but no trace of the cable car survives. You can still get a bird's-eye view of the Devil's Dyke – provided you have the skill, and the nerve, for this is a favourite spot for hang gliding. I wondered what the inhabitants of the 'impregnable' fortress would have made of humans hovering bird-like overhead. Hang gliders had been left on the grass like resting peacocks and they attracted the attention of a herd of cattle. They sniffed at the strange objects, until one became entangled in the wire and panicked, galloping across the turf, giant wings dragging along behind him. I wondered if I was about to witness the first ascent of a gliding bullock, but he soon got free. So I set off instead down the steep face of the scarp for the pleasant village of

The curved iron end of a shepherd's crook forms part of the gate to Pyecombe church. It was manufactured in the nearby forge.

Fulking where I was spending the night. The path emerged beside the pub where a perpetual spring gushes out into the road. It was this that brought the village into being and, at one time, thousands of sheep were brought here to be washed every year.

The next morning opened with blue skies, sunshine, and birdsong – which all lasted for as long as it took me to finish breakfast and, by the time I had set out for the climb back up the escarpment, the cloud had settled down with an air of dull permanence. The path leaves the edge to pass round the back of the hills, depriving the walker of the chance to see the scant remains of the Norman stronghold on Edburton Hill. At Freshcombe Farm I joined a minor road that led past the oddly suburban-looking youth hostel, before dropping down into another of the main river valleys, that of the Adur. The most prominent landmarks are provided by a vast cement works sitting at the foot of a quarry and the rather stark silhouette of Lancing College on the hill above Shoreham. But matters closer to hand were not without interest. A footbridge took me across the river to the hamlet of Botolphs. There is not much of it, but the church shows Saxon features and, when I went inside, I found an arcade blocked off, so at some time, there must have been a far larger congregation. Outside you can see the marks in the fields, the remains of an old village that has shrunk to a hamlet. At some stage in its history, Botolphs suffered a catastrophic decline in population, probably as a result of the Black Death, and never recovered its former importance. The few who stayed, however, prospered, though there is an interesting contrast in styles between Annington Farm and its grander neighbour, Annington House. The former is a vernacular building roofed with sandstone 'slates', which come from the Weald and are known as Horsham stone. The roof is essentially plain, but weathering and colouring by mosses and lichens have provided a rich texture. The big house, in contrast, presents a well-ordered, if somewhat stiffly formal, Georgian frontage to the world.

The climb from the valley was not, for once, along an open path but up a sunken lane, shaded by trees, more suggestive of the West Country than Sussex. It did not last, and soon I was was back with the wide views, dominated now by the isolated bulk of Cissbury Hill, its flanks notched by the now-familiar silhouette of ramparts that mark it as an Iron Age fortress. It remained in view for a long time, so I had ample time to study it. From certain angles it presents a somewhat pock-marked face, as though it had been shelled. If I could have risen above it and looked down, the effect would have been even more pronounced. This is no battleground, however, but what one might call one of the country's earliest industrial sites. Neolithic man soon found that some flints could be worked better than others and, though there are flints in plenty to be picked up on the ground, the best often lie in solid layers beneath the surface. So he dug a pit down to the flint using antlers as pickaxes and animal shoulder blades as shovels and then tunnelled outwards into the flint. It was not possible to travel far from the central shaft, so when one shaft was finished it was abandoned and another begun. In time, the shafts caved in, leaving deep hollows – our distant shell holes. At Grimes Graves in Norfolk, it is possible to go underground in a similar flint-mining area.

Cissbury Hill lies to the south of the downs, but up ahead was one of the most famous landmarks along the way: Chanctonbury Ring. It is not the feature itself that is so outstanding as to dominate all the surrounding countryside. It owes its prominence to a gentleman named Charles Goring who, as a young boy in the 1760s, carried seedlings up to the hilltop, watered and tended them, and lived to see them grow into a crown of mighty beech trees. They are visible for many miles – indeed they were still in sight when I reached the end of the South Downs Way. The trees mark a spot which is of considerable interest in its own right. As I walked towards it, I found the way crossed by shallow dykes, and I found that the trees themselves lay within a ring marked out by earthworks. This could hardly have been a defensive wall, since the ditches would scarcely trouble the progress of an energetic toddler. It is officially described as a fort, but the earthworks suggest a definition of property as much as a defence. In the centre of the ring, excavators discovered the scant remains of a Roman temple, a case of adaptation of an ancient site of presumed deep significance, not unlike the placing of Alfriston church on its prehistoric mound. It seemed an appropriate place to pause, eat lunch, and muse on the workings of history. Here was a Roman temple on an even older site, set beside a track that was probably in use thousands of years ago – and today it is no more than a useful stopping place for walkers, travelling for the sheer enjoyment of the open-air life.

I left the ring, crossing another set of earthworks that guarded the approach path and walked down to one of the dry valleys that cross the route and up the other side, for a long, steady slog through the fields. At least I had the reward of fine views across the Weald to the distant, hazy hills. Here there are marks on the land which are not always easy to interpret. To the south of Kithurst Hill, a long bank topped by a hedge stretches out straight as a rule, but a large-scale map provides the revealing information that this runs exactly along the line of a parish boundary. At Rackham Hill the way is crossed by a deep ditch and banks, which seem to be associated with the just-discernible shadows of

*The South Downs Way
leading up to the tall beeches of
Chanctonbury Ring.*

*A field of poppies beside the
South Downs Way at
Jevington.*

The deep inner ditch and ramparts of Maiden Castle.

Chalk cliffs near Durdle Door, Dorset.

an old pattern of fields. It may have been a way of separating off grazing land from arable, but it seems a somewhat extreme answer to the problem. It does not seem to fit in with other boundaries, nor is there any obvious settlement to be defended. Yet it is certainly a structure on a far grander scale than any of the other cross dykes met along the way. Perhaps one should not be too surprised to find that not every mystery comes complete with a solution.

The next valley is the broadest met along the way and contains the most important river, the Arun. With the construction of the Wey and Arun Canal in the early nineteenth century, it formed part of a waterway route that stretched all the way from the English Channel to the Thames. Its days of glory are sadly gone, but there are memories of former grandeur. The old flood plain, the Wild Brooks, remains virtually empty of buildings but, where the higher land licks out a dry tongue towards the marshes, the towers of Amberley Castle can be plainly seen. My path, however, headed further south towards the narrowest part of the valley and the bridge across the river. But first, the pathway took to a road which balances on a narrow ridge between two deep chalkpits and, if you peer through the protective screen of trees to the south, all kinds of intriguing things catch the eye – including some fine, narrow-gauge steam locomotives. This is the home of the Amberley Chalk Pits Museum, and those with time to spare should certainly pause, for there is much to see. I have paid more than one visit, and there always seems to be something new on show. On this occasion, however, my thoughts were rather more clearly focused on the Bridge Inn and a pint at the end of the day!

The next day I strolled across the bridge to look down on the river and its protective flood banks. It is not difficult to see how, in the days before metalled roads and motorized transport, navigable waterways were far and away the best means of moving goods from place to place. The alternatives were the high chalky paths of the downs or the clinging mud of the Weald. I, however, faced a steady but unremitting climb from my position down at sea-level to the summit of Bignor Hill, 224 metres (737 feet) above me. The view back showed the huge bites that had been gnawed out of the hill above Amberley, while up ahead was the woodland which was to become an ever more important feature in the landscape as I walked on towards the west. On Westburton Hill, a sign pointed off announcing a path to the Roman villa, which suggested there might well be interesting things waiting up ahead.

A little way beyond the Toby Stone, a mounting block set as a memorial to a fox-hunting gentleman and his wife, there is a break in the trees which provides a glimpse of the Roman villa, solitary among the

The deep, natural valley, the Devil's Dyke. The flattened top to the the hill on the left marks the site of an Iron Age fortress.

fields. The buildings are modern covers for the ancient remains, but it is just possible to see a grid of lines in the grass which are the foundations of Roman walls. It is distantly interesting, but closer at hand is a more intriguing sight: a pair of tumuli stand out clearly in a field, the dark green of the rough grass contrasting with the paler shades of the crops, and beyond that a great circular patch of the same rough grass. A path leads down towards it marked by a curious signpost pointing to Londinium, Regnum, and other Roman towns – curious because, although we have already seen signs of Roman settlement, there is nothing up here to suggest any Roman influence whatsoever. So, forgetting Rome for the moment, I made a deviation down the track to the south to investigate the grass circle. Close to, it can be seen to be marked out by a low bank. We have come right back to Neolithic man, who created this simple ring some 5000 to 6000 years ago. It is known as a causeway camp, a name which suggests that people lived here, though no evidence has ever been found to support the view. Another suggestion is that this was a stock enclosure.

Returning to the main track, I soon found that the Roman signpost had come a little too soon. A flat-topped embankment runs across the line of the walk and, from the map, you can clearly see that it is part of a straight track, continued in places by footpaths and in others by roads, running in a south-west to north-easterly direction. This is Roman Stane Street, joining Chichester (Regnum) to London and this is one of its most interesting sections. Here you can see how the road was built on a bank, or agger, with drainage ditches on either side. It was once a good deal wider, but weathering has eaten it away to the present width – the distance between the ditches giving a more accurate measure. Excavation has shown that it was built up of layers of chalk and flint,

They look like toy trains from a child's model railway but are, in fact, part of the Amberley Chalk Pits Museum collection of narrow-gauge industrial locomotives, glimpsed from the South Downs Way.

with broken flint and gravel as a top surface.

Woodland encroached ever closer to the path which, on a day of gathering clouds, seemed on the whole to be a good thing: and, for once, the timing of the weather was immaculate for rain and trees arrived simultaneously. The shower over, I walked, or rather slid, down to the A285. It is easy to make wrong assumptions on a walk. Having marched downhill on a broad chalk path, it seemed logical to march on uphill along the broad chalk path opposite. It was only when I had panted my way up to the edge of Charlton Forest that I became suspicious. I checked the map and, sure enough, I had come the wrong way. There was nothing for it but to go all the way down and start up again on the right line, a faint track across a grassy field. Then this path, too, disappeared into the woodland. Underfoot, the path changed from chalk to sticky clay, while the dense forest seemed all enveloping. All sense of being on an upland walk was temporarily lost. The official South Downs Way guide notes that the area is of interest to entomologists, which I take to be a polite way of saying that you will be plagued by flies. The woodland, however, is not devoid of interest. I noted a bank and ditch forming a boundary – a method of marking out woodland that has been in use for hundreds of years. This was certainly no new boundary, for mature trees now grow on top of the bank. Nevertheless, I had a feeling of relief when the woodland opened out to the north – and a pleasant surprise for I came upon a pair of fallow deer. The clumping of my boots soon sent them scampering back to the cover of the trees. After that there was only the descent to Cocking for my last stopping place before the end of the way.

The last day began, as had every other, with a steady climb out of the valley, but with the comforting thought that when I reached the top of Linch Down, I would not have any higher summit to reach. The path, unlike the one I had followed the previous afternoon, offered wide views over a Wealdland landscape that smoked with early mist. That, however, came to an end on Treyford Hill where not only did I again find myself on a narrow track hemmed in by woodland, but woodland bounded by a high wire fence topped with barbed wire, a sort of rural concentration camp. The inmates are not humans, but exotic birds, whose harsh, unmelodic calls seemed quite out of place in the Sussex countryside.

There was a temporary break in the woodland with fields to the right of the path, but up ahead where it again plunged into the trees, I could see the outline of tall grassy mounds. Once I got into the woodland, I found a track that led to the mounds, which were as one could have guessed, barrows. But these were on a far grander scale than any I had seen on the rest of the walk. There were six tumuli in a row, which are known locally as the Devil's Jumps. They are bell barrows, each surrounded by a ditch, and excavation showed them to hold cremation remains. The hollow in the second barrow of the series marks the nineteenth-century investigation.

If the wooded areas had so far been rather dull, the next section more than compensated – a lovely mixed wood dominated by giant beech trees, the undisputed kings of the downland forests. The route now swung round Pen Hill in a wide semicircle, with Beacon Hill rising up ahead. A ridge joins Pen Hill and Beacon Hill, but it is cut by earthworks, forming a switchback walk along the path. This was the first real indication that I was approaching another hill fort. The official South Downs Way skirts the foot of the hill, but it is far more interesting

An idyllic end to a long-distance walk: old cottages stand beside the village pond at Buriton.

to charge straight up the steep slope to the summit. I soon realized that the hill itself was the best defence against attack, steep and taxing, which may explain why the ramparts that crown the summit seem somewhat insignificant affairs. When I did reach the heights I found myself on an extensive plateau with views opening out in all directions, a complete 360-degree panorama.

The South Downs Way had nearly ended and, down below, I could see the spire of South Harting church. I was tempted to miss out the last couple of miles and simply settle for the Iron Age fort as a fitting climax to the walk, but when it came to the point I simply could not do it. To come so close to completing a long-distance walk and then not to reach the very end was simply impossible. So I strode past the ruined stone tower of Tower Hill, down a tree-shaded lane, and on along a rutted track. Perseverance brought its due reward, for looking back it seemed the whole range of the Downs was laid out for inspection, right back to the unmistakeable crown of beeches on Chanctonbury Hill and beyond. The actual official end of the walk arrives at the county boundary but, as that is unmarked, the nearest point when you can really claim to have done the whole thing is indicated by a huge copper beech tree that stands by Sunwood Farm. Even that, however, is little help as far as rejoining the rest of the world is concerned so I walked on to Buriton, across the fields of grazing sheep, past prosperous farms to a shady spot where the parish church looks down over the village pond. It seemed a quintessential old English scene but, if the walk had done nothing else, it had shown me that such a scene is really quite modern when set against the whole timescale of human history in these islands.

FORTRESSES AND FIELDS

Corfe Castle to Dorchester, 29 miles (47 km). OS maps 194, 195.

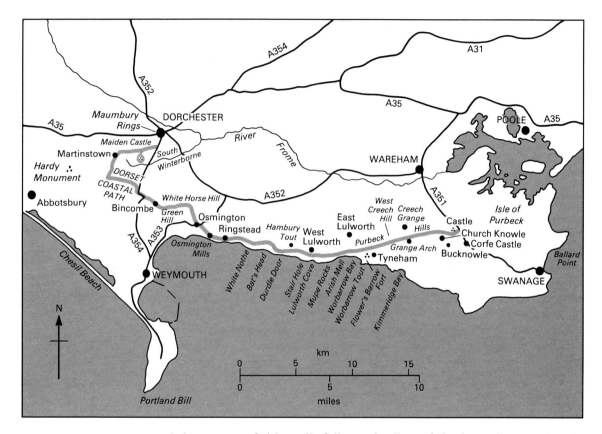

A large part of this walk follows the line of the long-distance Dorset coastal path but it begins inland in the Purbeck Hills. These hills form an almost continuous chalk ridge, stretching from the coast at Ballard Point to regain the sea near Lulworth Cove. The area to the south is known as the Isle of Purbeck. Why island? The answer to that appeared soon after I started walking. There is one principal gap in the hills, providing easy access to Purbeck, and it comes as no surprise to find a castle guarding this strategic point. This is Corfe Castle, and town and castle together have become one of the most popular holiday attractions for tourists hunting out the picturesque. They also form what seems to be a very obvious pattern for one form of early English development. Here was a point to be defended so here, raised up on a high hill, are the tall castle walls while in their protective shadow the town grew and prospered. In fact, the story begins earlier than the stone walls might suggest, for there was a wooden Saxon tower here before the Normans came, and even the present castle is the result of a long period of development. William the Conqueror established a castle here; Henry I built the stone tower which is such a prominent feature, and the whole structure was extended by King John. It was a Royalist stronghold in the Civil War, and suffered the inevitable fate of a fortress occupied by the losing side. Yet even in its ruins it retains a good deal of its old grandeur.

The village to the south spreads out in a V from the base of the castle hill, and it is if anything even more romantic in appearance than the castle. The V shape left a space in the middle for a market, while the houses gradually extended out along the two arms. The buildings are of stone with stone-slate roofs, and offer a clue to Corfe's prosperity. Purbeck was once famous for its limestone, a good building stone as the houses testify, but it was also a stone that could take a high polish, earning it the name 'Purbeck marble'. It became very popular with church architects and the trade flourished in the sixteenth and seventeenth centuries which is when many of the fine old houses in the town were built. It all makes for a satisfying pattern: the castle at the gap, the water mill standing by the river at the foot of the castle hill and the market town spreading out from its base. It is a classic pattern of town development. Yet we are looking only at a pattern of comparatively recent development, for this area can boast settlements that go back more than 1000 years before the Norman Conquest. My main object in this walk was not to look for glimpses of British life at the time of the Norman Conquest, but to look further back to the time when those earlier conquerors, the Romans, reached these shores.

After a stroll around Corfe and its castle, I set out to walk the ridge of the Purbeck Hills towards Lulworth Cove, but here a word of caution is necessary. This part of the walk crosses the Army firing ranges and can only be used when the range walks are open.★

There are numerous alternative routes between Corfe and Lulworth but I opted for the high-level path which is reached from the road that curls around the north side of the castle hill. Just beyond the bridge across the stream was a bridleway sign pointing up the hill. As I walked up this path, the nature of the ridge was clear for, on a sunny day, the chalk surface was shining up a brilliant white. I was fortunate enough to be walking on one of those beautiful May mornings which seem to be overtures to summer – though only a week earlier I had been walking by the Rochdale Canal in snow! I was grateful for the fine weather for, as the South Downs walk had made clear, such steep chalk paths become slimy, slithering, and grey in the rain. Stone and flint showed through

★This information is available from The Range Officer, RAC Gunnery School, Lulworth, Dorset. In general, the walks are open most weekends, the whole of August, and Bank Holidays.

Corfe Castle rises high above the village streets. The village is famous as a picturesque beauty spot, and much of its attraction derives from the use of the local Purbeck stone.

the chalk and the former had been put to use. On the hillside beside the path I could see the ruins of a lime kiln. In its working days, the kiln would have been loaded with a mixture of limestone and a suitable fuel, and burnt to make lime which could then be used as a fertilizer.

Once I had reached the top of the hill I could see the length of the ridge, a great hump, stretching east and west, dividing the land. I could look down on both sides, but first I looked along the ridge itself for signs of human activity. The chalk upland carries something of the same message as the South Downs Way. The thinness of the soil is obvious from the manner in which the path has worn through to the chalk, so that one would hardly expect anyone equipped with an efficient plough to think it worth scraping away at this poor soil. So, the prominent reminders of the distant past remain undisturbed: a lone round barrow providing a link back to the Bronze Age. I made the point before that the presence of graves for the dead cannot be taken as conclusive proof that there were homes for the living in the same place. The ridge is covered with a mixture of grassland, where sheep were grazing, and patches of gorse. The wildlife of the area clearly showed the same delight in the weather as myself: birds sang a cheery chorus, with the lark taking the leading soprano role; early butterflies tested their wings in the sun. A solitary kestrel hovered above the valley where little, it seemed, excited its interest. The bird remained on station, almost motionless, with just an occasional flutter of the wings to preserve its stillness.

Below the steep slopes of the ridge, there is a quite different story to be read. You can see how Purbeck came to be known as an island, for the sea can be seen on either side, stretching its blue sheet to the faintest of horizons, where it meets the paler blue of the sky, while, to the north, the wide bay of Poole Harbour sends tongues of water licking into the land. This is a flat landscape of marsh and rough heathland, where isolated farms mark the occasional areas of higher, drier ground. The land to the south is very different. Here is a rich, green area of villages and fields in a chequered pattern, marked out by hedgerows. Groups of houses and farms can be seen, surrounded by large rectangles, which are not at all like the regular, square fields of the enclosure movement of the seventeenth and eighteenth centuries. You can see this pattern

Two of the main aspects of medieval life can be seen here: the castle representing the feudal power of the Norman lords; and the water mill at its foot standing for the agricultural life of the surrounding area.

round Bucknowle and Church Knowle, the latter easily distinguished
by its prominent church. What I was, in fact, looking down on was a
pattern of Saxon estates, a landscape the essential elements of which
were already well established by the time of the Norman Conquest. One
can see the attractions of the area for, even from up here on the ridge,
its lushness appears in marked contrast to the scarred, chalky ridge and
the wasteland of marsh and heath behind it. Down there are the
limestone quarries and the arable land, based on the rich, heavy band of
Kimmeridge clays which lies in the bowl between the Purbeck Hills and
the cliffs that mark the sea's edge.

Walking westwards along the ridge, you can measure the poverty of
the soil, for even the patches of woodland seem to have little to offer
apart from wretched, stunted trees. At Cocknowle, quarrying has sliced
at the roundness of the hill to expose the chalk, and the evidence of how
close the chalk lies to the surface seems to have been an inspiration to the
locals, who have added their own names and initials to the landscape.
Then the view to the north was lost, closed off by the Great Wood – and,
when the view opened up again, it brought something of a surprise. A
curious pinnacled archway appeared on the horizon, quite alone, with
no signs of any other buildings around it. A recent acquaintance with
Corfe Castle might lead to a first impression that this was part of another
defensive position on the hills, but there are no signs of decay, and the
stones of the arch are all regular, unworn by use or time. This is Grange
Arch, a folly and easy to interpret. If you stand in the central arch and
look down the hill, you find yourself staring straight down an avenue cut
through the woodland towards a grand house at the bottom. But this is
to see everything back to front. The idea was not to provide a view of the
house from the hill, but to supply an interesting focal point for the
people in Creech Grange when they looked up at the hill. This is an 'eye
catcher', a popular device at the end of the eighteenth century, when the
picturesque movement was at the height of its popularity, and landscape
gardening very much the latest thing. The ideal was to have a romantic
ruin to view from your windows, and, if the genuine article was not
available, you faked one – hence Grange Arch.

The path diverges from Great Wood to give clear views across the
land to the north. I looked down on a jigsaw pattern of fields – some the
regulation, squared-off patterns of enclosure, others marked out in a
bewildering variety of irregular shapes. This is the eastern edge of the
wasteland and has been worked from a very early date. It is impossible
to be precise, but this is a landscape where the patterns of cultivation
were already established by the time Domesday Book came to be
written, and the local name, Creech, is of Celtic origin. But it is later

land use that dictates where you walk now, for this is Army territory. Throughout the year, shells are lobbed into the hills, not all of which explode, so that warnings about keeping to pathways need to be taken seriously. This also means that you need to make sure that you really are on the path you intend to take for, once set off along the wrong route, there is no way to cut across country to the path you meant to follow. I had no problems, however, in keeping to the waymarked footpath that begins by the car park on the top of West Creech Hill. It is, admittedly, a touch frustrating to be limited to a narrow corridor, but the sight of the twisted remnants of shell casings alongside the path are a more than adequate deterrent to straying from the official way.

The military presence is felt in all kinds and varieties of ways. The land to the south looks as rich and pleasant here as elsewhere. I could see a tower overlooking Kimmeridge Bay, another folly built for no other purpose than to give its owner a pleasant view. It seemed something of a misnomer to refer to such buildings as 'follies', for what could be more sensible than to build a pleasing tower to obtain a still more pleasing view? At first, there seems no obvious difference between the region to the east and to the west of this tower, yet it is close to this point that the boundary falls. And as I walked on, so I could see the effect of the Army takeover in the tumbled, ruinous buildings that were once the village of Tyneham and its surrounding farms. The village was acquired by the Army as a 'temporary measure' during World War 2 for troop training and never returned to the original residents. But the need to prepare

This odd structure, looking vaguely like an accidentally preserved remnant of some medieval building is Grange Arch. It is, in fact, a folly designed to provide a focal point of interest in the scenery.

for war is no new phenomenon in these parts, for evidence of far older preparations soon appeared on the crest of the ridge. Earthen ramparts marked the beginning of Flower's Barrow Fort. The artificial nature of the works was immediately apparent: the ditch cutting across the line of the ridge and its accompanying wall of chalk and earth are typical of Iron Age hill forts. This one is far from complete, much of the southern perimeter having collapsed, but enough remains to show that these were substantial fortifications. The fort stretches over a wide area of the ridge, and there are other ditches to be seen which could well have been outer defences. It was a stronghold which was eminently defensible, and which could provide shelter for a considerable population. But the question which the fort cannot answer is – what kind of people lived here and how did they make a living?

The walk began at Corfe Castle – a fortress providing protection for a local population who farmed and quarried. The Iron Age fort had a similar role, and it is possible to see that the similarities do not end there. The steep land to the north of the fort has some very significant marks on the ground, ridges that divide the land into roughly square areas. This is a so-called 'Celtic' field system. Here the people of Flower's Barrow used their primitive ploughs to scrape and turn the thin soil to grow crops. The ridges are the lynchets, of a type seen first from a distance during the South Downs Way walk. As an area of sloping ground is ploughed, so the earth will tend to fall towards the downhill side, where it will accumulate to form a low bank. Here, where the fields are set at an angle to the ridge, lynchets form on all four sides of the field. Today, such systems can only be seen in areas such as this, where the soil is too poor to attract the attention of modern farmers. The lynchets remain like fossilized remnants of a field system where crops were grown when Flower's Barrow fort was new, more than 2000 years ago.

Beyond these field marks, the army of today is busily creating its own landscape, which might well prove equally intriguing to walkers of the future. Shell holes pit the hillside while, out on the plain, the tanks have carved sinuous tracks which, from a distance, look like the traces left by a mob of giant, demented worms.

The path now runs towards Worbarrow Bay, its eastern end marked by the great rock comma of Worbarrow Tout. The descent was abrupt, a foretaste of things to come, a knee-jolting drop down to Arish Mell. It also, somewhat depressingly, gives all too clear a view of the path climbing just as steeply back up to the ridge on the far side of the inlet. There is, however, a consolation prize for the expenditure of all this effort, for the cliff scenery becomes ever more splendid as you go along. Limestone forms an initial barrier to the sea but, where the sea breaks

The true nature of Grange Arch becomes clear when you look through the central arch. An avenue through the trees brings the arch into the view of the residents of Creech Grange, down below in the valley.

Worbarrow Head. Here one can see how the sea has, over the centuries, eaten away at the soft chalk to produce this typical Dorset coastline of high cliffs and rounded bays.

through, it soon eats its way into the softer chalk to take huge scoops out of the land. So you find the cliffs forming round the semicircle of Worbarrow Bay leaving outliers, such as the Mupe Rocks, as remnants of the hard, limestone ridge. The land swoops and dives between the bays, so that the whole coast looks like the edge of some monstrous hand saw.

Up on the next ridge, Bindon Hill, yet more earthworks appear, not at first glance as spectacular as Flower's Barrow. But, as I walked on, I began to appreciate the extent of the fortifications, which look like an attempt to enclose the entire promontory between Lulworth and Mupe Bay. I was still looking at the work of Iron Age Celtic people, who probably began the work somewhere around the fifth century BC. After Flower's Barrow you might expect another field system but, for a while, the constrictions of the range walk make it impossible to see down the slopes. Then, just before Lulworth Cove was reached, I arrived at the limit of the army ranges. What a relief it was to be able to wander and explore at leisure. How sad it seemed that this, some of the most beautiful coastal scenery in Britain, should be closed off to the public. But what is bad news for us is good news for the wildlife, which seems unperturbed by regular bombardment; good news, too, for the plants that grow untroubled by pesticides, fungicides, or any other 'cides'. And, to some extent, it is good news for the historian. Shells may make holes, but harrow and plough cause far greater damage to the faint marks that are all we have to tell us about the farming landscape of prehistoric times.

Alongside human history, there is a natural history that moves at a very different pace: both can be seen at West Lulworth. The natural phenomenon is the obvious attraction. Here the sea has again broken through the limestone barrier and eaten away into the land, this time producing an almost perfect circle of blue water – Lulworth Cove. Alongside you can see where it is happening again. Once more the sea has penetrated the armour crust at Stair Hole and is beginning to gnaw its way into the softer flesh of the land. Infinitely slowly, the coastline is changing, so slowly that the remains of human efforts to shape the land seem of quite recent origin. But it was these that I went to see next, able at last to roam across the north face of Bindon Hill to see the lynchets of the Celtic fields. It seemed an appropriate place to end an afternoon's walk along the Purbeck Hills. The way led down to West Lulworth and the village pub – but over to the west, a broad white stripe of chalk up the steep green hill warned me of what I could expect the next morning.

Coming out of West Lulworth, I opted for the gentle route round the back of Hambury Tout to Durdle Door. The village of West Lulworth is nearly a mile from the sea, which might seem a little surprising because the cove offers one of the few sheltered anchorages along this coast of high cliffs. But, as I climbed the hill, I had fine views over a wide downland landscape and I realized that this was the world to which West Lulworth belongs: the world of agriculture, of sheep grazing the uplands, and fields of grain, not the world of sea and fishermen. But the sea is becoming increasingly important to the area, for it now brings in a new source of revenue – holidaymakers. The area south of Newlands Farm is now a huge caravan and camping site. We tend to take it for

The classic case of the power of the sea. Having broken through the outer edge of the hard limestone, the sea has gnawed away at the chalk to produce the almost perfect circle of Lulworth Cove.

granted that people want to come to the seaside, yet this is a comparatively modern notion – and the reasons for coming have changed. It began in the eighteenth century when sea water was thought to have unique medicinal properties. The robust swam in it, others had it brought to their rooms where they solemnly sat in a bath of it, and a few even drank it. Sea bathing for fun did not begin until the nineteenth century, while the twentieth century has brought its own variation – lying down beside the sea to get a tan. The caravan park is, after all, a part of a changing historical process, just another example of how people use the landscape.

Durdle Door is a much-photographed, popular spot. Once again, we find the limestone jutting out from the softer chalk, where the sea has battered the exposed rock to carve out a tall archway. From here, the path dives downhill again to a narrow, L-shaped valley which leads back towards Newlands Farm and which shone out with a brilliant green spring growth against the startling white of the chalk cliffs. Farmers have to make the best they can of the arable land today, just as they did in the past. This lesson was made plain once again as I trudged up the hill at the back of Swyre Head. The best route to follow to see the ancient farmland is via the path signposted to 'The Warren' which curves away up the hill to the west. There in the shallow dip that stretches away from the coast at Bat's Head, I could see shapes that might just possibly have been particularly wide pathways cut into the hillside. These are, in fact, strip lynchets; not at all the same thing as the lynchets of the Celtic fields, but broad cultivation terraces carved out on the steep hillside. This type of field system is usually thought of as being medieval, but these terraces might well be of an earlier date, a variation of the system seen on the Purbeck Hills.

Walking along the top of steep cliffs backed by rough downland, most people are content just to walk and enjoy the scenery – and I am certainly no exception. It was certainly a day to enjoy, with a cloudless sky and an unruffled sea that seemed as motionless as crumpled silk. The water stretched out to some unidentifiable horizon, and I had little company other than the soaring gulls riding the currents in the warm air. A solitary raven threaded its way down a rocky valley. But, inevitably, my curiosity was aroused. What is that obelisk on the hillside? Not as it turned out a monument but, quite literally, a landmark, or to be precise, one of a pair of landmarks. These are shown on marine charts, so that when a look-out on a passing ship has the two marks in line, then he has a completely accurate bearing. He will know just how far along his course he is, or he can take a bearing of his own and test the accuracy of the ship's compass. This might seem a little odd

The so-called 'Celtic fields', which date back to the Iron Age, are distinguished by lynchets, ridges of earth that mark field boundaries, and which are formed by the downhill movement of earth loosened by the plough.

to walkers who are used to assuming that compasses are accurate instruments, but adding or moving metal around on a ship will change the compass reading. Quite recently on a trip down the west coast of Scotland, I found that metal work done on board had produced a 7-degree error in the compass reading. Such marks then have a practical use, if not for walkers then for those who sailed the seas in the days before radar and satellite navigation systems.

The map itself provided the next intriguing puzzle. The area to the west of the row of cottages at White Nothe is called 'Burning Cliff'. It might make sense if the rocks were bright-red sandstone, but there is nothing in their appearance to give even a hint as to the origins of the name. In fact, you have to turn back to the history books to find the unlikely answer that the name is not a figure of speech but a description of an event that actually occurred. Rocks contain a variety of minerals, and beneath these cliffs there is an oily shale and iron pyrites, a sulphide

Durdle Door, the spectacular arch carved out of the cliffs by the sea.

of iron. When the latter oxidizes it gives out heat, and in 1826 that proved enough to set the oil on fire. The cliffs literally burned, and continued to burn for a whole year.

The burning cliffs marked the end of this stage of the walk by the sea, for now the path came down to the wide sweep of Weymouth Bay, where the high cliffs disappear. There is a geological change of direction, for I had left the limestone region to enter a broad band of clay. The limestone could be seen reappearing in the distance as the rocky island of Portland. The path now led me past a straggle of holiday homes to a large field ringed by woodland. Once there was a village here, the village of Ringstead, as a useful information board beside the path tells you. Nothing, however, is visible from the track but, if you walk into the field, then the remains start to appear as ridges and hollows. They are by no means easy to distinguish, and it takes a practised eye to follow the line of a ridge in the ground to see how it delineates the shape of a house. But, if you concentrate hard, you do begin to see how the ridges trace the collapsed walls of houses, with gaps which represent doorways. Usually, on such deserted medieval village sites, hollows will represent street lines, but here the pattern has been complicated by later drainage ditches. It is a pattern that could be seen much more clearly from the air than from the ground. The obvious questions are, why and when was the village deserted? There are no clear answers but records show that Ringstead church had ceased to function by the end of the fifteenth century, when all its functions were taken over by neighbouring Osmington. We do not know if this was no more than an official recognition of the fact that there was no longer a village left to serve, or whether it was a mark of a shrinking village, and the movement of the church to Osmington simply accelerated a gradual process. The why is even more speculative. Local tradition has it that pirates raided the village, burning, looting, and murdering, and that the locals who fled never had the heart to return. It is a colourful story. Another popular explanation for desertion of villages lies with the ravages of the Black Death, but records show that, although many villages were tragically reduced by the plague, few succumbed totally. Alternative theories include a great loss of life among the fishermen of Ringstead in some especially violent storm. We shall probably never know. But what struck me in walking around this village, which is now little more than a shadow on the ground, was just how little remained after such a comparatively short time when measured on the scale of history. The thought helped to give perspective to consideration of the traces of ancient fields and hill forts, abandoned not just centuries but millenia before Ringstead. Seen on that timescale it seems a miracle that anything from so remote a past can be recognized when the recent past can seem so bewildering.

The storm theory is given some credence a little further along the coast where pieces of rusted iron rise up like the skeleton of some sea beast above the waves. They are all that remain of the SS *Minx*, stranded on the rocks in 1929. If a disaster such as this could overtake a modern steamer, it is not difficult to imagine the effects of a gale on a fleet of wooden fishing boats. The path now dropped down almost to the beach to reach Osmington Mills and the Smugglers Inn. Here, it is claimed, a

These slight traces of dips and mounds in a field are all that remain of the medieval village of Ringstead. The depression was once a village street, while the mounds were cottages and houses.

medieval building lurks, but it has been all but submerged beneath modernizations and extensions. What you have instead is a bright and chirpy seaside pub doing a brisk trade to the accompaniment of Radio 1. It is not to everyone's taste but, after a morning's walk in the hot sun, I was happy enough just to see a row of beer pump handles on top of the bar and the well-stocked food counter.

At this point the Dorset Coastal Path divides, one branch keeping strictly to its definition and following the coastline round through Weymouth, the other providing an inland alternative that eventually regains the sea at Abbotsbury. I chose the latter and followed the road out of Osmington Mills for a short way, before cutting across the fields to Osmington. For many people, Corfe Castle represents the ideal of a Dorset village, but the unspoiled quiet charms of Osmington have at least as strong an appeal. Osmington owes such importance as it has to the arrival of the Normans. This was originally Osmund's Town, named after the nephew of William I who was granted the manorial rights as duly recorded in Domesday Book. Osmund was an important man in his day, the founder of Salisbury Cathedral, though there is little in the village to hint at his importance. The church at the top of the village street sets the mood: nothing ostentatious here and, although it was heavily restored by the Victorians, many original features were left, including the Perpendicular tower and the beautifully proportioned chancel arch. For once, one can talk of genuine restoration and not of a rebuild of a plain church into a gothic extravaganza. The houses set on either side of the main street that winds down the narrow valley are equally appealing. They have an air of belonging precisely to this landscape, with their plain walls of local stone and thatched roofs. There was once a rather grand Tudor manor here, but all that remain are the ruined walls and one massive door in the churchyard.

The village street peters out into a lane that climbs up to White Horse Hill. No problem here with nomenclature, for carved in the hillside is the horse and its cocked-hatted rider, said to be a representation of George III, and cut into the chalk during his reign. It seems an odd thing to find above an old Dorset village, until you realize that you are standing on a hill commanding views down to the coast at Weymouth, and George III was a frequent visitor to the seaside town. The white horse was Weymouth's way of saying thank you to the king who had helped to make their town into a popular resort. But, as I climbed steadily up the path to the ridge at the top of the hill, so Georgian England disappeared from view and older landscape features were reasserted. In fact, the next half-dozen miles (10 km) were to offer a tremendous concentration of ancient sites.

The white horse of White Horse Hill carries the figure of George III. The king was a regular visitor to nearby Weymouth and his patronage brought a good deal of cash to the region, hence this monument.

These began to appear almost as soon as I reached the top of the hill, the characteristic rounded humps of ring barrows standing out in sharp contrast against the chalky white of the fields. There were over a dozen of them, laid out more-or-less in line along the path that headed towards Green Hill. There was clearly a pattern in their placement, but there is now no way of discovering its significance. There is, however, a certain logic in the notion that the dead were greatly revered so that, not only were their bodies covered by impressive mounds, but those mounds were set in the most prominent site that could be found, at the top of a high ridge. It is always possible that other barrows down in the valley have been ploughed over and simply vanished from sight, but here the concentration is so great that I felt that this must indeed be a Bronze Age graveyard, deliberately planned. The idea gained in strength the further along the walk I went. But even the barrows could not hold my attention once Chalbury Hill came into view. Even from a distance, it was obvious that I was seeing another Iron Age fortress, for the earthen ramparts circling the hill stood out with great clarity. Here, instead of the partially preserved fortifications seen in the Purbeck Hills, was the complete thing, and very impressive it looked, too. With the line of tumuli behind me and the fort up ahead, I really did have a strong sense of stepping back into the past – and, most importantly, a populated past. It is sometimes difficult to picture the way of life of people who lived their lives so far back in history, but already this walk through Dorset had introduced me to communities who planted crops, cared for their dead, and were prepared to defend themselves against aggressive neighbours. Two of the elements were on display at this one spot and, as I walked on towards Bincombe, the third element reappeared if in somewhat more modern guise.

The downland path came down to a road which was followed for a short way before the track reappeared heading up over Bincombe Hill.

Strip lynchets could clearly be seen carved into the hillside, long terraces following the contours of the hill. Once, this whole hill was common land, and the lynchets represented the only means by which it could be divided up for farming. The Bincombe fields were probably worked in this way as early as the eleventh century. Now the lynchets are under grass for, early in the sixteenth century, the grandest of the local landowners applied to have the downs enclosed for sheep rearing. He was opposed by his tenants and, though the records of the dispute are incomplete, the outcome is obvious: sheep now graze where crops once grew. It is difficult now to imagine the passions generated in that distant conflict between landlord and tenant, sheep and plough, for most of us now have only the most tenuous connections with the land. The pylons that cross Bincombe Hill bring electricity to the towns, so that our supermarket lamb can be popped into the electric oven and our wrapped bread slipped into the electric toaster.

Bincombe itself shows little sign of dramatic change, a peaceful village that climbs the steep hill above the church. Bincombe church is, if anything, even plainer than Osmington's, but they did give it a new wooden door at the end of the eighteenth century and carved in the date when they finished it. The coastal path now turns north at the top of the village, but I wanted a last look at the Bincombe fields, so I carried on to the main road where an even more impressive set of strip lynchets could be seen. I had to pay for my interest in ancient farming techniques by a trudge up the main road, busy with weekend traffic. The modern road bends out into a sharp elbow to ease the gradient up the hill but, when I regained the official walk, I found myself on a track that continued the straight line, regardless of hills. I was, in fact, following the line of the original Roman road to Dorchester, which was going as straight as Roman roads are supposed to do. Whether this assumption is true or not is something I would be discovering on the next walk.

The path now headed off westwards towards the Hardy monument, erected not to honour the writer who made Wessex famous, but for the other Thomas Hardy, the admiral who was with Nelson on the *Victory* at Trafalgar. This final ridge of downland offered a superb climax to one theme of the walk, for it was lined with round barrows, set so close together that there were always one or two in view at any point along the way. The other theme of hill forts reached an even more crashing crescendo, for the northern horizon was dominated by the grandest of them all, Maiden Castle. It is possible to take a direct line down to the site along the B3159, but I preferred to keep at a distance for a while. Maiden Castle is so big, so impressive, that it is not always easy to take it in as a whole. From up here on the ridge, however, I could see how the hill commands a wide tract of ground, looking out over the valley of the Frome to the north and rising above the Winterborne valley that separates it from the ridge to the south. Strategically, it can hardly be faulted.

Meanwhile, the ridge led on westwards and, at the end of a day's walking, when the sun had turned me lobster red, I ticked off the tumuli on the map like so many prehistoric milestones. Here one really can say that it cannot have been an accident that devised the line of mounds so that they dominate the skyline. Perhaps, as in so many old religions, the people of the time saw the sky as the home of spirits and brought the dead to the high places to give them a start on their journey to the next world. Or perhaps, literally, they wished to look up to their ancestors. What does seem indisputable, however, is that they indicate a quite heavily populated countryside, with a distinct and distinctive culture. The view of the distant fort gives rise to another idea, that as the Bronze Age gradually gave way to the Iron Age around 500 BC, so the pressure of population would have been increasing. This made it necessary for a tribe to defend what it had against the encroachment of neighbours. The messages of this landscape tell of protection for the living as well as reverence for the dead.

The final stage for the day arrived with the path down to Martinstown, which seems the odd man out as far as names are concerned, for the other villages in the Winterborne valley all carry the name of the river. In fact, the name is a modern contraction, as this was originally Winterborne St Martin. The path down to the village brings a scattering of barrows and a reminder that even here below the ridge, the soil is often no more than a thin layer above the chalk. A small quarry carved out of the hill shows a cross-section of the land – and is a useful source of material for such jobs as surfacing the path along which I was walking. Martinstown is, as one might expect, a long, straggling village, its shape determined by the narrowness of the valley. It has grown in recent years, with the addition of new houses that have taken note of the styles and materials of the old village and which, as individual houses, blend in most happily. When so much thought and care have gone into this aspect, it is sad to find that the same attention was not given to the overall plan. In an essentially linear village, the new houses loop off in a little crescent, borrowed from suburbia.

The last section of the walk brought me to Maiden Castle itself. It is a short walk in terms of distance, little more than a mile (1.6 km) as the crow flies, but it seems to take an eternity to reach the outer ramparts. I took the easiest route leaving by the road that turns northwards at the end of the village and then taking the footpath through the Clandon

Estate, and quite suddenly it was there, looming over me. I was glad of the long diversion on the previous day, for Maiden Castle is simply too large to comprehend in a single glance when it is right on top of you. But here at least I could really appreciate the grandeur of the work: the depth of the ditches, the height of the ramparts. The western entry shows the care that went into making this what the builders clearly hoped would prove an impregnable fortress. To pass through the complex defences that crown the hill I had to take a convoluted course, overlooked for every step of the way by high ramparts. Attackers who survived that obstacle course would originally have been confronted by gigantic wooden doors that guarded the final entrance. How could an assault succeed in an age when weapons were limited to the throwing spear and the sling shot? Quite simply, it could not succeed.

When I reached the plateau, I was faced by an apparently featureless expanse of grassland, stretching off into the far distance. In fact, the fort covers an area of 18 hectares (45 acres), so what we have is not a castle at all in the sense that we usually think of the word, not something at all like Corfe Castle. This is a defended settlement, for which a more accurate modern analogy would be a fortified town. As you walk round the perimeter, you find that Maiden Castle is built not on one but on two hills, with a definite dip in the middle and, if you head in towards the centre along the line of the dip, then you find the whole place is much more complex than at first appears. You can now see another shallow ditch and slightly raised bank, stretching around the edge of the more easterly of the two hilltops. It has no obvious function in relation to Maiden Castle as we see it now and, if it is a defensive work, then it is on a quite different and much inferior scale. What you are seeing here, in fact, is the outer limit of an earlier settlement on this hilltop site – one built not just a few years earlier but started right back in Neolithic times, somewhere between 3000 and 4000 BC.

Maiden Castle remained for centuries as a comparatively simple causewayed campsite, protected by shallow, concentric circular ditches. Then, around 300 BC, the great works we now see were begun. The main fortifications were dug around 150 BC and the complex entrance mazes were constructed around 75 BC. There is not a lot to see that tells of the life of the castle, though there is a pit near the edge of the Neolithic camp that was once used for grain storage. One puzzle remains unsolved: where would the people of the castle get water in times of war? For without water supplies, they could hardly have withstood a siege for any length of time. But if that question remains unanswered, we do at least know what happened when Maiden Castle faced its greatest threat. In AD 44, the fortress lay at the heart of a

An aerial view of Maiden Castle. At the bottom of the picture is the complex pattern of ramparts that mark the eastern entrance. The fort can be seen to have a division across the centre: the lower part was the original Neolithic fort. The square enclosures near the southern rim are the site of the Roman temple.

territory controlled by a British tribe, the Durotrigians, and it was here that they gathered to await the arrival of the Roman legions under Vespasian. They had stormed through southern England, but even they were brought to a halt by this formidable fortress. The British had prepared for the battle. Thousands of stones had been collected from nearby Chesil Beach and piled up ready for the slings of the defenders. It would have been enough to turn back any of the armies that could have been brought here by the neighbouring British tribes, but the Romans presented a wholly new threat.

I walked round to the eastern end of the fort, where it was plain that

The henge monument of Maumbury Rings in Dorchester was adapted by the Romans and used as an amphitheatre.

the defensive labyrinth of the entrance is less complex and less daunting than that at the west. It was here that the Romans staged their assault. Their weapons were infinitely more sophisticated than those of the defenders, weapons such as ballistae which were used to hurl missiles; these were to sling shots what a field gun is to a pistol. The old technique of raining down stones on the attackers had worked in the past, but now the defenders faced a new phenomenon. The legionaries linked their shields above their heads and advanced under their cover, as well protected as a tortoise beneath its shell – and this was the name given to this formation, the testudo or tortoise. The result was inevitable, and Sir Mortimer Wheeler in his excavations of the site in the 1930s found sad reminders of the British defeat. Outside the eastern gateway was the war cemetery, each dead warrior supplied with meat and beer for his journey to the next world, and one skeleton was found with a Roman bolt still embedded in his backbone. This somewhat grisly relic is preserved in Dorchester Museum.

In a sense, the story is not dissimilar to that of Corfe Castle where a fortress designed for the warfare methods of one age succumbed to the superior tactics and more sophisticated weaponry of another. And, in both cases, the castle was slighted by the victors, its defences reduced to make sure that it would never again pose a threat. The difference at Maiden Castle lies in the fact that here there was not merely a clash between different ages but between different civilizations. The British had about as much chance of standing out against the forces of Rome as the bow-and-arrow-carrying American Indians did of preventing the westward march of settlers armed with guns. The defeat of the British did not prove to be quite the last act in the story of Maiden Castle. Three centuries later, when the country was again being attacked from all sides – by Picts and Scots, Franks and Saxons – the Romans came back to the fortress and built a temple. You can still see its foundations and the outline of its walls in the north-eastern corner. Here excavators found statuettes to the gods of both the cultures that had made war here two centuries before: there was a three-horned Celtic bull god and the Roman goddesses, Minerva and Diana. It would seem that help from any quarter and any religion was welcome in the face of the new threats. Maiden Castle is a place that encourages one to linger, but eventually I had to walk back down through the great western entrance and out on the road to Dorchester.

The suburbs have nothing to differentiate them from those of any other large town, but the past is at least remembered, if a touch incongruously, in the first street names that I met – Forum Green, Caesar Green, and, to keep a balance, Celtic Crescent. The Romans set up their own fortress on the banks of the Frome, which, over the years, was to develop into the town of Durnovaria, modern Dorchester. As I reached the main road near the town centre, I walked past the cemetery and the railway bridge and, by a busy main road junction, I saw a high grass mound. This was to be the end of my walk, a place where the very ancient past and the Roman world met. When I reached the mound I found it to be hollow, a giant grass doughnut with two entrances. It is known as the Maumbury Rings and is, in fact, a henge monument dating back like the first fort at Maiden Castle to the Neolithic period. The Romans, however, saw it not as an ancient monument or as a site of deep religious significance, but as an ideal spot to adapt as an amphitheatre. The old was incorporated into the new. The Romans who had come as soldiers stayed as settlers and brought new standards of civilization to Britain. And that will be the theme of the next walk.

THE ROMAN ROAD
Cirencester to Chesterton, 40 miles (64 km), OS maps 163, 164.

During the last walk, we saw something of Rome at war: the theme of this walk is largely Rome at peace, even though the story begins with the conquest of AD 43 to 47. The invasion stemmed less from a desire to add Britain to the Roman empire, and more from the desire of the Emperor Claudius to consolidate his own position at home. Military success overseas was, and still is, a useful way of diverting attention away from shortcomings at home. Nevertheless, the campaign was successful, and by AD 47, Rome had control over a large part of the country. A frontier was established, protected by forts, and along that frontier a military road was constructed, the Fosse Way from Exeter to Lincoln. A fort was built close to a major settlement of the Dobunni tribe and, as peace became more securely established and Roman rule extended further north, so the frontier fort grew into a town. It took its name from the British Caer-Conym, meaning highest point, for it lay on the River Churn, highest tributary of the Thames. It became the civitas or capital of the Dobunni. So the name of the town was Corinium Dobunnorum,

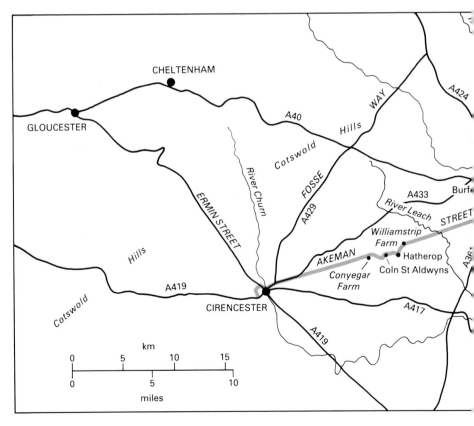

later anglicized to Cirencester. It was the meeting point for a number of roads: Fosse Way, Ermin Street, and the road I was to follow, Akeman Street. The latter was not built to ease the movement of legions dashing off to trouble spots, but as a trade route designed to feed the new Roman prosperity. But before setting off along the road, we can take a look at what remains to give us a hint as to the power and importance of the Roman city of Corinium.

I started my walk, literally, in the middle of Corinium, which in modern Cirencester means the junction of Tower Street and Lewis Lane. The town was originally laid out on a regular grid pattern and, here, the four main streets leading to the four town gates met, though there is little in the modern town to indicate this. In fact, the most impressive Roman remains in the area lie at the edges of the old town boundaries, and that was where I was heading for my first stopping off point. I walked off towards what was once the south-west gate which stood at the junction of present-day Querns Lane and Sheep Street. The

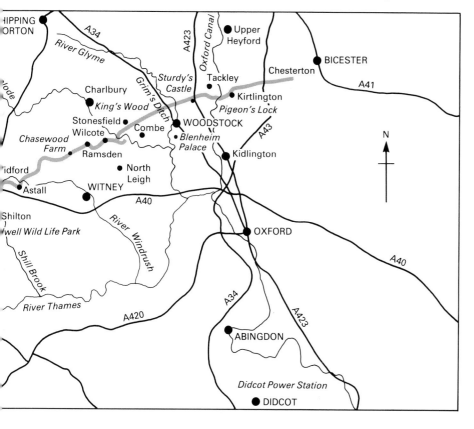

The Roman road of Akeman Street, still preserved as a minor country road, running between hedgerows bright with flowers.

Roman road then headed straight on out of town, but the modern bypass has closed off that route, so that I had to make my way round the edge of an industrial estate to cross the busy dual carriageway. The latter at least gives a clue as to what lies ahead, for the deep cutting has exposed the layers of limestone on which the town stands. Turning up Somerford Road and Cotswold Avenue, I saw a tall obelisk which announces the entrance to the site of the Roman amphitheatre.

At first, everything seemed merely a confusion of disturbed ground, and what looked very much like a set of overgrown spoil heaps – and this, in fact, is exactly what they are. They are the remnants of a Roman quarry: the rock so evident in the new road cutting, was dug from here to build Corinium. In front of me, one mound rose up, at once higher and shapelier than the rest. Once on top, I could see that the bank was one of a pair that curved round towards each other to enclose the arena and the amphitheatre. Between the banks are the entrances, which were aligned with the road through the south-east gate. Once these banks were terraced to provide seats for spectators, and if you can imagine that scene, then you will see that what you have here is something that would look exactly the same as a modern athletics stadium. This is not too surprising because this was indeed a place for sports meetings, though it was used for other entertainments as well – much as Wembley Stadium is used for the occasional pop concert. It is a big arena with seating for several thousand spectators, and provides a first clue to the size and importance of Corinium.

I chose a route back which largely followed the original line of the town walls as shown by excavation – though little enough remains in view. The route runs north up Sheep Street and Park Lane and round into Thomas Street to the Abbey Park. But though there may be little to see of the Roman town along the way, there is a good deal to show the continuing prosperity of Cirencester as it developed through the ages – and a short diversion takes you to the excellent Corinium Museum. The principal appeal of the museum lies with its superb preserved mosaics, of which more later, and its careful reconstruction of the main features of the Roman town: not, as they say in the adverts, to be missed. Along the way, one is struck by the profusion of good seventeenth- and eighteenth-century houses, mostly built of stone. The best houses have ashlar fronts, that is, they are faced with dressed stone blocks, smoothed by masons. Craft work of this standard does not, and never has, come cheap, so it is another measure of Cirencester's historical affluence. Individual buildings show more of the history of the town. The fifteenth-century Weaver's Hall is a clear indication that the early prosperity of Cirencester was built on the wool trade, based on the sheep that grazed the surrounding Cotswold Hills. There is a suggestion, too, of the ecclesiastical importance of the town in the remains of St John's Hospital, founded in 1133 by Henry I, primarily as a resting place for travellers. All one can now see are the arches of the former chantry, a row of charming cottages occupying the main hospital site. But most impressive of all is the majestic parish church with its richly decorated porch and tall tower. The latter is not quite so sturdy as it appears, hence the heavy buttressing which had to be added after completion. Inside, for those who divert from the Roman walk – and it is hard to resist the temptation – is a light, airy, yet richly decorated church.

The main walk now brought me to the park, the site of Cirencester's dominant abbey. Even less remains of this than of Roman Corinium. There is the Norman gate and the abbey pond, but elsewhere all you can see is a neat, tidy municipal park. However, between the lake and the river there are swellings in the ground and, as I walked round the lake, so I found the slight swellings developing into a recognizable bank. This is the actual Roman wall. This half circuit had at least given a notion of the size of the ancient town – once only second to London. Restoration has now given us a chance to see something of the fabric of the city wall. At first, a clay and gravel bank was the only defence but towers were added in the second century, and in the third century, the bank was cut back to allow a stone wall to be constructed. Here you can see just how well the work was done, with ashlar blocks comparable to those of the best town houses. In fact, in many cases they were the same blocks, for the good citizens of Cirencester found the stone wall of Corinium to be a useful source of ready-cut, made-to-measure building blocks.

From here I made my way out of the park, down London Road and through the vanished north-east gate on to the A433 stretching straight ahead – the Roman road that was to divide between the Fosse Way and my route to the east, Akeman Street. The turning off the main road bends through a right-angle, but then turns back again to pick up the Roman route. If you look forwards, you see the expected straight line of the original road, and if you then look behind you, you can see how the Roman road is still clearly marked out by the line of the field hedgerow. However much modern road engineers might deviate from the line of their distant forerunners, the old route is seldom entirely lost. Even so, the niceties of alignment are by no means easy to discover. Does the modern route, with its bends that ease the gradient of the hill represent the original Roman line, or did the earlier route follow the traditional straight line up through the accompanying woodland? There is simply no means of telling by direct observation.

One of the problems faced by walkers trying to follow an ancient route is that not one but several generations of road engineers have imposed their notions on the system. Woodland appeared by a crossroads, its boundary marked by a beautifully constructed dry stone wall. Such structures are true works of art, though construction in this part of the world is easier than in some other parts of Britain as the Cotswold limestone splits off into neat, rectangular chunks. Nevertheless, to see a wall such as this, where each individual stone has been selected and positioned with care, perfectly balanced to keep the wall strong and firm, is still one of the visual treats of the countryside. But such walls are more than that for, as well-defined boundaries, they offer a hint at least that our modern road is following a long-established route. So when you see a road falling between such clear lines, you can start to make tentative guesses as to how it has, or has not, changed over the years. Here I found the tarmac to be little better than a narrow strip running down the centre of a wider avenue marked out by walls and ditches. It is now a decidedly narrow route, not even achieving the status of a B road, but it looks very much as if it might once have been

Akeman Street following a zigzag route across the Leach valley.

The village of Shilton is centred on this ford on the Shill Brook.

Opposite *The massive, upright stones of the Ring of Brodgar.*

A puzzle for the historian. The modern road on the alignment of Akeman Street bends to ease the gradient on the hill, but did the Roman original have a less dramatic curve as seen in the hedgerow on the right or did it run straight?

A stone milestone with a cast-iron plate is a survivor from the days when the old Roman road received a new lease of life as a turnpike road in the age of stage coaches.

a good deal more important, even after Akeman Street fell into disuse. Confirmation appeared soon enough in the grass verge opposite a small farm. A milestone stands, almost lost in the tall grass, but still bearing a cast-iron plate announcing that I was now exactly 4 miles (6.4 km) from Cirencester. This part of the story was now very clear, for the cast-iron plate dates from a period that began towards the end of the eighteenth century, the great age of turnpike roads. It is not unreasonable to say that this was the first time that British roads were even half as good as those laid down during the years of the Roman empire. A new generation of engineers provided firm, decent, well-drained surfaces which were a boon to road users – though they had to pay for the privilege of using them, much as motorists in Europe have to pay to leave the old main roads to take advantage of the modern motorways. The road builders collected the revenue, but the law decreed what they must provide in return and, among the benefits which they gave to travellers, were signposts and milestones. This road

must have seen many changes in its fortunes, veering between importance and obscurity. It is its present obscurity – a minor road with scarcely width for two cars to pass – that has preserved the evidence of the older routes.

Looked at on the map, it might seem that the modern route and the Roman road follow identical tracks for many miles but, on the ground, differences soon begin to appear. The builders of a later date were not quite so obsessed as the Romans with ruling mathematically precise lines on the landscape. Drivers of horse-drawn carriages were not too keen on charging straight up and down every hill, and much preferred the easier gradients that came with a curved route. Bends occur on the new road but, where they do, you can usually see the original line still defined by hedge and wall, and it is at such spots that it is easiest to pick out the distinctive features of the Roman original. Straightness is the one characteristic one always associates with the Romans, and the easier gradients of the modern road do help to show how enthusiastically they pursued their goals. But this was not just a product of blinkered, bureaucratic thinking, but a sensible use of available resources. Surveying is a complex art, but laying out straight lines is simple, given sufficient manpower, which is the one thing the army had. No special

The handsome, Gothic-styled gatehouse marks the entrance to the extensive Conyegar estate.

equipment is needed except a lot of men carrying tall sticks, which can be lined up with total accuracy, by ensuring that at any one point there are always three in a straight line.

The straight line is easily seen, but what is not so clear is the method of construction. The Roman road was a good road, for the Romans were aware that the secret of success lay with good drainage. So they built up their roads on embankments, known as aggers, which sloped away on either side to ditches. They then built up the road surface, using gravel or larger paving stones, on top of the agger. There are glimpses of the agger, particularly at the points where the modern route diverges from the ancient way. Near Conyegar Wood, my road swung south, and the Roman line appeared only as a crop mark, a dark-coloured line across the bordering field. But when an unploughed section appeared, the agger could clearly be seen, standing proud above the ground. I kept as close as I could to the original by following a footpath across the Conyegar estate. The entrance to the park is clearly marked by a splendid lodge, with an ornate Gothic doorway emblazoned with a coat of arms. The path passed Conyegar Farm, sheltering behind a protective semicircle of trees, and then headed off down to the valley of the River Colne. Sadly, the crossing point on the river is on private land, but this is such a delightful, lush river valley and so full of interesting features that it seems churlish to complain at the loss of just one, solitary feature of antiquarian interest.

The waters of the river divide, one stream meandering off through meadows while the other is controlled by sluice gates. The latter is an artificial waterway, cut to divert a part of the river water, and I expected to find it finishing up at the water wheel of a mill. I was still some way from the village, but this is a very gently sloping valley so, if the mill stream was to get up a good head of water, then it would need to be started some way from the mill itself. My path followed the line of this mill stream or, leat, passed through a wood and then emerged by the second of the Conyegar lodges but, along the way, the stream showed more evidence of its artificial nature in little weirs and waterfalls. There are tantalizing glimpses of rich Cotswold stone houses, suggesting that Coln St Aldwyns might well be a place to linger. When the village did appear, the first thing I got was confirmation of the chain of evidence collected along the way, for there indeed was the mill, straddling the water and announcing its old function by the millstones propped up outside. It is always most satisfying to have a theory so resoundingly proved. I felt quite smug, and rewarded myself with lunch at the village pub.

The village is as charming as one could hope, and there is a splendidly

This building at Coln St Aldwyns would proclaim itself as a mill even without the millstone as a clue, for the mill stream and the prominent loading doors are conclusive evidence.

anachronistic notice on the post office, announcing that the services provided included money orders, savings bank, parcels, telegraph, insurance, annuity, and express delivery service. The road now wriggled along to the south of Akeman Street, with a view of an extraordinarily grand establishment, a positive riot of pinnacles, gables, and towers. Nearer at hand, was a quite magnificent dry stone wall and another leat leading off from the river, not this time providing power for a water mill but for a pump house, lifting water up the hill. The grand house commands a fine view from its hilltop position, but still relied on the river valley for its main services. The great houses could afford such luxuries just as they could afford to house the estate workers. Hatherop village displays the characteristic uniformity which shows that all was the work of one guiding hand. It is a planned village where everything dates from the second half of the nineteenth century, but has been given a suitably quaint, old-world village appearance. There is still room here for the occasional quirky detail, such as a sundial built into a chimney. The surrounding country, too, shows the mark of planning – neither wild country nor cultivated country, but a sort of halfway compromise. This is a carefully organized landscape, arranged to give an impression of naturalness but in which every visual effect is stage-managed. In the midst of it sits a handsome Georgian mansion, but the days of the great house are not what they were. The old walled garden now contains a modern housing estate.

I rejoined Akeman Street at Williamstrip Farm, the home farm for the big estate and an extremely fine place it is. The house is particularly pleasing, retaining its Georgian proportions which manage to suggest a natural unity even though the house has clearly been altered and extended over the years. Its charm lies in good measure with the use of local materials, such as the stone slates on the roof, and the same use of appropriate materials spreads out to the farm buildings and barns. On a more modest scale, farmworkers' cottages offer the same comfortable, almost cosy harmony with the natural world. No discordant notes are struck here, for even the woodland offers a fine selection of old, mature trees, with rich colour tones ranging from the bronze of the copper beech to the floral candleabra of the horse chestnut.

At the start of the drop down to the valley of the Leach, Roman road and new road again part company, but here it was possible to keep with the older route in what turned out to be one of the most interesting sections of the entire road. Having dwelt at some length on the straightness of Roman roads, here was the exception to prove the rule. the Romans were no fools and they were as conscious of the need to

Akeman Street takes a curved line along the hillside as it drops down to the crossing of the River Leach. Here it can still be seen clearly as a hollow way.

avoid over-steep gradients as any modern engineer. Here was a case where the straight line would have been totally inappropriate. The Roman road can easily be seen, starting as a hollow way sweeping round in a curve to the valley bottom which it crosses on a very pronounced agger, before heading across towards the woodland on the far side of the modern road. The route was easy to follow now, across the fields and on to pick up the surfaced road again. A tree-shaded avenue provided an evocative image of a road somewhat nearer to the heart of the Roman empire, while that somewhat foreign air was enhanced by strange cries from the animals of the Bradwell Wild Life Park.

Again old route and new diverged, as the new bent south to reach the village of Shilton. The village itself centres round a natural ford on the steep-sided little Shill Brook. It is a delightful spot, and it is worth a detour to see the church and churchyard. In the latter you can see one of the local 'woolpack' tombs, gaining its name from the shape of the packs of wool from the Cotswold sheep. It was the wool trade which made this area prosperous in the days when wool lay at the heart of the English economy. Just north of Shilton, a footpath leads off the Burford road and intersects with Akeman Street. It is a momentary encounter which could easily be overlooked. A hedgerow, ruled revealingly straight, joins the path beside the ruins of a dry-stone shelter, crosses, and continues on its way. The footpath itself leads eventually to Widford which, as the name suggests, was originally a fording place on the Windrush. The path shows ample evidence of age-long use in its bordering stone walls and the mature hedgerows, the latter sporting a rich variety of bushes and shrubs. And for a moment I even believed that I had returned to the familiar signs of ancient history that had marked earlier walks for, up ahead, the land rose up in shapely mounds. But it soon became clear that these were not tumuli nor barrows, but simply spoil thrown up from a modern quarry.

After the quiet of footpaths, the A40 arrived with a roar which one is inclined to regard as a noisy intrusion into a quiet contemplation of the past. Yet the Romans would surely have approved; a fast, well-built road designed for efficiency, not picturesque beauty. It offers few pleasures, however, for those on foot assailed by noise and fumes, and the few hundred metres of main road down to the junction with the line of Akeman Street were quite enough for me. In theory, the line now continues as a public footpath, which heads through a small triangle of woodland to Asthall. In practice, only those with the perseverance of a Stanley in search of Livingstone will bother to pick a line through the fields of grain and attempt to make a way through the dense thickets. It is far easier to take the minor road and, in doing so, you will miss

nothing of note. At Asthall itself, however, there is no shortage of interesting detail.

The valley of the Windrush is a delight. The river wanders slowly through rich meadowland, and any newcomer would be happy to settle on its banks. The Romans certainly found it appealing, and a settlement grew up around the crossing, about a quarter-of-a-mile (400 metres) from the present village. It is easy to see why Asthall and its Roman predecessor are now some way apart, for the more recent settlement is centred not on a busy transport route, but on the raised ground that overlooks the river. Here are manor house and church, the former proclaiming its wealth and affluence to the world in gables and battlements, the latter preserving its finer points for the interior. The church certainly comes as something of a surprise for, although its architecture shows the familiar pattern of aggrandisement of a plainer Norman foundation, later additions have given it a startlingly colourful

Asthall church and manor house. The tomb in the foreground with the rounded top is shaped to represent a wool pack, a reminder that the prosperity of the manor was built on the wool trade.

face. The walls and ceiling of the chancel are covered in paintings which look suspiciously like pastiches of medieval styles – which indeed they are. The north transept has an even grander visage, with a huge, richly carved arch covering a recess in which is a memorial of a lady, dog at her feet, stonily contemplating eternity. But, for me, the most satisfactory monument was the plain, simple stone altar with its piscina, the small basin where the communion vessels could be washed. Everything else in the village is subservient to manor and church, but the place as a whole proclaims its importance by the avenue of trees that shades travellers on the road past the edge of the village.

As Asthall has moved away from the site of the Roman settlement, so the road out of it is very much a wandering English road, in marked contrast to the severely straight Roman route. It crosses the Windrush on a pleasant, modest stone bridge and then proceeds to wind between high banks and tall hedgerows. I was still on the fringes of the Cotswolds but there were changes to be noted in the scenery. Patches of dense woodland, isolated remains of the great Wychwood Forest, dot the landscape. Buildings, however, still show the same characteristics of golden stone walls and stone slate roofs.

Akeman Street reappears as a bridle path beyond Field Assarts, a name which repeats the message already clear from the landscape itself, that in this area the farmland was carved out from the forest, for 'assart' means an area of private land cut out of the common woodland. But, with the return to the Roman road, the scenery changed yet again – to a flat, open airy landscape with wide views across the Oxfordshire plain dominated by the distantly smoking chimney and towers of Didcot Power Station. The path passes through a meadow of tall grass, clover, and wild flowers which one might think of as a throwback to an early age of agriculture, but which the ruins of buildings and the all-but-invisible straight tracks of tarmac reveal to be an abandoned airfield. Soon, no doubt, these few traces will disappear and the World War 2 military installation be no more prominent than the ancient road. Further along, a group of chestnuts forms a protective ring around Chasewood Farm and here the old road reappeared as something more substantial than the line of a cart track. A distinct mound marks the track of the agger. Its old function as a transport route has long gone, but later generations found it a convenient field bank and planted a hedgerow along the top. Once the modern road is reached, however, the old function returns and the road carries on as straight and true as a Roman road should be all the way to Ramsden.

Ramsden itself has little to offer – a war memorial, a somewhat dull and drab Victorian church, and it has contrived to swallow up Akeman

Street. I was forced into a detour through Wilcote, which again has little of interest to show beyond another nondescript church, the grange and Wilcote House, hidden away discreetly in its park. The road did once go through that park, and the name derives from the original Anglo-Saxon 'Wicham' indicating a Roman settlement. None of that can now be seen, but only a mile (1.6 km) away is the Roman villa of North Leigh. Here one gets a glimpse into the way of life of the small communities served by Akeman Street. The villa was by no means unique. This was what a Roman estate agent would no doubt have referred to as a prime site for development. The soil is rich, well watered by the nearby Evenlode, and an excellent area for growing crops. It lies off the edge of the Cotswolds and is spared the worst of the weather that blows across the stony scarp – yet the Cotswold grassland is still near enough for grazing flocks. The virtues of the area were recognized before the Roman conquest, for a Belgic farm once occupied the site. It was a rich area, and it was to tap that richness that the road was built. Once it was completed, villas such as North Leigh spread along its line. The wealth of the land can be seen in the wealth of the villa itself.

The remains of the hypocaust or Roman central heating system at North Leigh. Hot air from the furnace was channelled through these ducts beneath the floor.

The first impression I received was of size, even though the walls now scarcely rise above their foundations, and not all have been uncovered. The name 'villa' nowadays tends to suggest a rather cosy, suburban

Above left *Part of the bath house at the North Leigh villa. This area was a part of the hot bath.*

Above right *A decorative pavement in the Roman villa at North Leigh. The geometric pattern is the work of a school of mosaicists at Cirencester.*

house, but this was really a large farm estate, with grand rooms and superb facilities for the owners, and ranges of buildings for the servants and animals. The whole complex contained some sixty rooms surrounding a courtyard. It was a place of considerable opulence, and if not cosy in the suburban sense, then certainly everything that could be done to make the occupants comfortable was done. The most obvious signs of wealth are the mosaic pavements, of which the finest is that in the fourth-century dining room. It was the work of the mosaic school based in Cirencester and, if its geometrical patterns are not quite so exciting as the pictorial pavements on show at the Corinium Museum, it is still very impressive. The designs are intricate, the craftsmanship involved in setting the tiny coloured fragments in place that go to make the mosaic, superb. You need no written documents to convince yourself that the people who lived here were wealthy and sophisticated. There were sixteen rooms in all boasting fine mosaic floors and a further eleven with plain tessellated floors. Outward show is, however, only a part of the story.

The Romans of North Leigh prized their creature comforts. The heating system at the villa was not only efficient, it was a good deal more efficient than any system that the people of Britain were to see until well into the twentieth century. The simplest form was the channelled hypocaust: hot air from a furnace was circulated through channels beneath the pavement and then escaped through hollow tubes built into the walls of the room, so that the hot gases almost surrounded the living area. In the pillared hypocaust, the whole floor was raised up on pillars, so that the entire surface was kept warm. In other words, this was an underfloor central heating system, to which the Romans added good insulation. But the most impressive feature was the bath house – or rather bath houses – for Roman bathing was no mere dip in a soapy tub. They went through a whole series of rooms, starting with the apodyterium, or undressing room, and then progressing through rooms of ever increasing temperature, before finishing of the whole process with a plunge in the cold bath. Bathing was a long and social occasion, not unlike a modern sauna, and the calderium or hot room near the entrance to the site has some of the best-preserved features. It has two apses, one with a tank for hot-water bathing. It is easy to imagine the Romans lingering there for a long chat. It is only a part of a large, complex site, yet somehow seems to speak particularly clearly of the wealth and luxury of Roman Britain at the height of its powers.

The villa was always more than a rich man's house for, around the quadrangle, there were also workshops, barns for animals, and a few reminders that a household, especially a large one such as this, needed a lot of running. Along the south-west range you can still see the remains of four ovens in what must have been a large and well-equipped kitchen. When and how did all this luxury decay and crumble? No-one can say for certain but archaeologists found evidence of a fire, and of squatters who lit camp fires on the fine mosaic pavements. The few scraps of available evidence suggest that the decline was swift and absolute in its severity. If one can draw an analogy with a later century and another conspicuous example of a wealthy house, it must have been rather as if I were now to walk on to Blenheim Palace, only to find vagabonds eating their meals off the finest paintings. And this was only one of eight known villas that stood near Akeman Street where it crosses the valleys of the Evenlode and Glyme.

It should be possible to follow the line of the river round from the villa to take the crossing due south of Stonesfield, but the area beyond the railway bridge is so overgrown and the thickets so dense that there is little pleasure in the attempt. I preferred to retrace my steps to the road and once again pick up the line of Akeman Street where it passes close to the villa – and then stay with the road, almost without deviation, to the end of the journey. I also found it brought another interesting example of how the Roman engineers coped with a difficult terrain. The river bends in a giant U that reaches to the foot of the hill on which Stonesfield stands. A deep valley swings away from the river almost precisely on the straight line along which the road is heading. The road comes down the hill almost to the river, but then curves off as a distinctive ledge following the contour up to a line that can be maintained along the side of the valley. So, with little fuss, gradients are kept easy and deviations kept to the minimum. The footpath which

Here Akeman Street appears as a clearly distinguished footpath across a field of grain. It is still possible to see how the road was built up above the surrounding land, with drainage ditches alongside.

follows the route of the road, is now the waymarked Oxfordshire Way.

One of the fascinations in walking the Roman road lies in seeing how its identity has been preserved over the centuries: sometimes remaining as a transport route, in other places reduced to nothing more than a field boundary, and the full range of these adaptations will be met over the last dozen miles. The road which was quite distinct in the little, steep-sided valley seems to get lost when you cross the Stonesfield-Combe road, but the footpath follows a hedgerow that takes an absolutely straight line between fields of grain. And, as I walked, I found the division between the fields becoming ever more distinct, with a stone wall and hedge crowning a wide bank and ditch. The bank is, of course, the last remnant of the agger. It must, in medieval times, have presented a considerable obstacle to the plough, for the bank would have been higher and wider, with a ditch on either side and the top would have been covered with slabs of limestone. The easy way out was simply to accept the road as a convenient boundary and, once established, so it remained. That this boundary has been extant for centuries can be clearly seen from the massive trees that stand on top of it, and the even larger and more impressive stumps. The true nature of the boundary was at least preserved in the name of the farm beside the way, Akeman Street Farm.

A rather more impressive boundary rises up across the line of the walk beyond the minor road north of Combe, a high stone wall that marks the edge of the great Blenheim estate. The wall is so high that no mere stile can be used, so a miniature staircase has been constructed up to the top of the wall and down again on the other side. This is, in effect, the more modern equivalent of the North Leigh villa: a grand house occupied by family and servants, and surrounded by a working estate of farmland, park, and managed woodland. The latter is the first item to be met. Here I was walking through a surviving fragment of the great forest where deer were hunted, a royal prerogative remembered in the name 'King's Wood'. The wood was later managed for timber and the estate still has its own sawmill and maintenance workshops at Combe – a curious example of nineteenth century belt-and-braces thinking, for power was supplied either by a waterwheel at one end of the complex or by a steam engine at the other. Within the park area, however, I found a far more formal arrangements of trees. These days it is common to find the name 'regimented' attached to the uniform rows of conifers growing in new plantations: here, however, the term is quite strictly applicable. Akeman Street passes straight across the line of the driveway that runs from Ditchley Gate up to the Column of Victory and beyond to the lake and Blenheim Palace. The great house is the work of Sir John Vanbrugh – but just how much of the design is his and how much should be attributed to his exceptionally gifted and highly professional assistant, Nicholas Hawksmoor, is uncertain. What is certain is that the parkland was laid out by Capability Brown. The driveway was originally intended as the main approach to the house, and the formal arrangement of trees that flank it are arranged in a very particular order. Each group represents one of the battalions lined up for the Battle of Blenheim of 1704, for it was the Duke of Marlborough's success in that battle which the palace was built to commemorate.

Blenheim Park is an artifice, carved out from the old royal hunting forest and then given order by Brown, whose most daring device was the damming of the River Glyme to create a beautiful, artificial lake. Given such widespread change, it is all the more surprising to find the Roman road still preserved as a recognized and recognizable route across the estate. It is not, however, the sole survivor from ancient times. A substantial bank represents one end of a system of bank and ditch, known as Grim's Ditch, which runs, with numerous interruptions, from here round in an arc to Charlbury. At its most impressive, the bank rises to a height of some 1.8 metres (6 feet) and is 6 metres (20 feet) wide, accompanied by a ditch of equal proportions. It was clearly a defensive boundary, but who built it and why and when are all questions to which no firm answer can be given. It certainly predates Akeman Street, for the Roman road slices through it. The likeliest explanation is that it marks a tribal barrier constructed at about the time of the Roman Conquest.

After the park, the way crosses the busy A34 and continues as a road across the Glyme. This is a very minor road now, but shows signs of having once been rather more important: the grass verges are wide, and the boundary walls set far apart. There is a subtle change in the landscape, for I had left the Cotswolds behind, and that change could be seen most clearly in the buildings. I was still close enough to the limestone country for the familiar brown stone to be much in evidence, but I had now reached the valley of the Oxford clays, and brick was starting to become quite prominent. Hordley Farm shows a handsome face to the world, and the extensive buildings are a mixture of brick and stone; and instead of stone slates on the roof, tiles have taken over.

At the end of the little road, the way was continued by a footpath where, perversely perhaps, the Roman road could be seen at its clearest. The path is some 6 metres (20 feet) wide and raised well above the surrounding fields, and, even when it disappears into a small wood, it still retains its identity. It emerges on the main Oxford-Banbury road by the hotel called Sturdy's Castle. This main road follows an obvious line along the top of the ridge that separates the valleys of the Evenlode and its tributaries from that of the Cherwell. It has been an important route since prehistoric times, and, when the Romans arrived, they paved the section that runs south from Akeman Street. Later, it was to be a turnpike road, and Sturdy's Castle is a survivor from the days of the stagecoach and the post chaise. This is still an important route, unlike Akeman Street which is here reduced to the status of a lowly footpath.

The area to the south of the path is particularly interesting, for it shows a landscape feature which is quite common in this part of the country. The fields have the appearance of giant, green corrugated sheets. They were once under the plough, and successive ploughing created a pattern of ridge and furrow. Then, at some stage in the past, they were changed from arable to pasture, probably, as now, to provide grazing for sheep. So the old ploughed fields were, one might say, fossilized, stuck for ever with the ridges and furrows left from the days of crop growing. But, to the north, there is a very different pattern, for this is the edge of Tackley Park which survives even though the manor house has gone. And between lies Akeman Street. How long has it formed the boundary? Well, the land surrounding Whitehill Farm was given to St Frideswide's Monastery in Oxford in 1004, and Akeman Street was chosen as the obvious boundary.

Now the route diverges, interrupted by the river Cherwell and two, comparatively speaking, modern transport routes – the Oxford Canal and the Great Western Railway. The Cherwell valley provided an easy route along which the two could make their way, because both canal and railway engineers needed to keep their lines as near as possible on the level. Neither could quite achieve their aims, for the British countryside rarely co-operates by lying flat on its back. So the railway comes across

Flight's Mill has been converted to an attractive house, leaving the mill stream as an ornamental feature and home to a family of ducks.

the valley on an embankment while the canal climbs steadily through a series of regularly spaced locks. Path and canal meet at a spot full of interest, Pigeon's Lock, an odd name which originates with the building at the lockside which was once a pub. Here, the river, too, is not allowed to continue undisturbed in its natural line but is divided by weir and sluice to drive the machinery of Flight's Mill. The mill is now a most attractive private house but you can still see the arch under which water flowed to turn the wheel. The lock itself is typical of the first generation of canal locks, built to take a narrow boat 70 feet long by 7 feet wide (21 metres by 2 metres approximately) with no space to spare. That seemed more than big enough to meet the needs of mid-eighteenth century transport but, as the process of industrialization gathered momentum, so inadequacies soon became apparent. The railway of the nineteenth century took over the trade of the canal of the eighteenth century, just as the truck is now taking over from the railway.

Beyond the canal is a big stone quarry which, in its time, provided cargo for the boats, and later was to send its raw material to the cement works, whose tall chimney dominates the skyline. The track now runs down to the village of Kirtlington. Here, once again, the Roman road forms the basis for a park boundary, Kirtlington Park, but also provides the line for a modern road which most satisfyingly behaves in true Roman fashion by running straight on for over 5 miles (8 km) to Chesterton. Another minor Roman road, Port Way, also headed north from Kirtlington towards Upper Heyford. There should be an appropriate climactic end to the journey at the Roman town of Alchester, but Alchester has gone, decayed and passed into oblivion as the Saxon settlement of Bicester grew nearby. Perhaps this is the true message of the Roman road. The invaders brought new skills, new technology, and new standards of almost unbelievably luxurious living to these islands – yet all we have left are the traces, pallid impressions of all that grandeur. Nearly 2000 years were to pass before Britain could boast a transport system that could match the Roman road network for efficiency, and the Oxford Canal is just one reminder of the new works that came in with the industrial revolution of the eighteenth century.

The Roman world did not vanish on the instant, but slowly crumbled and fell as Britain entered what we know as the Dark Ages. But was this really just a collapse into mindless barbarism, or was it the replacement of one culture whose course was run by that of a new which had its own, if very different, vitality? In the next walk, I shall be looking at a very different area with a very different history, and one which shows a continuous line of change that stretches from prehistory into the Dark Ages.

Pigeon Lock on the Oxford Canal. The name is derived from the lock-side house, which was originally the Three Pigeons public house. The boat leaving the lock is an adaptation of a traditional narrow boat of the kind that carried cargo in the working days of the canal.

STORIES IN STONE
Maes Howe to Evie, 30 miles (48 km), OS map 6.

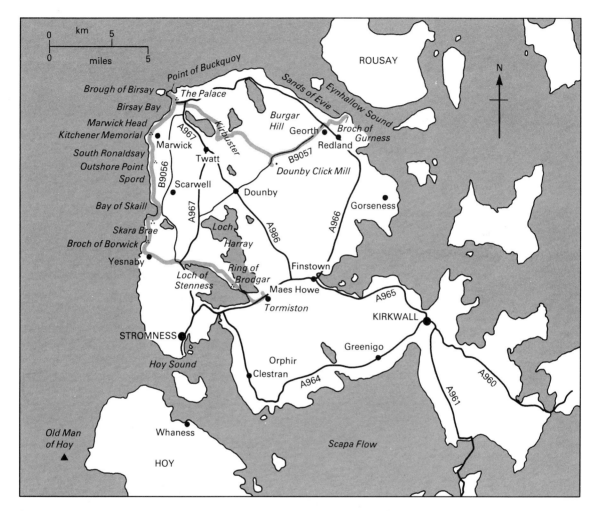

The simple act of leaving the mainland to travel to an island seems always to smack of adventure in prospect. One hopes that the island will be something more than simply a chunk of land, accidentally cut off from the rest of the country by a short stretch of water: one expects real, palpable differences. The traveller to Orkney will not be disappointed. And the magic begins even before you set foot on the islands, for the sea journey from Scrabster takes you past the giant cliffs of Hoy, sandstone ramparts that rise 300 metres (1000 feet) above the sea and which are coloured such a brilliant orange-red that, on a sunny day, they seem to glow. Shattered and splintered by wave and weather, they have retreated leaving solitary stacks, such as the famous Old Man of Hoy who did, indeed, once boast two strong legs. After that, landfall might have come as a disappointment, except that one is put down in Stromness, one of the most delightful towns in the whole of the British Isles. Stone houses rise above stone-flagged streets, where every alleyway offers its own special view – a glimpse of the sea and fishing boats, a paved courtyard and even, somewhat surprisingly, a sculpture by Barbara Hepworth. Once you leave the town the delights seem to multiply rather than diminish. It scarcely seems to matter where you go on Mainland, the biggest of the islands, or on any of its smaller neighbours, there is always something to grab the attention. The route I eventually chose was one which, in a sense, leaps furiously across time gaps that can be measured more easily in millennia than in centuries yet which, paradoxically, seemed to offer a particular unity. For the place itself determines how people should live here just as much now as it did 5000 years ago. So I began in the most distant past, at one of the most spectacular prehistoric sites in northern Europe, Maes Howe.

The first glimpse of Maes Howe took me right back to the round barrows, now familiar companions from early walks – but this proved a little misleading. The circular mound itself is very large and is surrounded by a broad ditch, which is not quite concentric with it. But what sets this apart from anything previously met along the way is the

The interior of the chambered cairn of Maes Howe, looking towards the entrance passage. The picture shows how the slabs of stone have been overlapped to form a roof. The workmanship makes this one of the finest Stone Age monuments in the world.

interior of the mound, for this is a chambered cairn in a quite extraordinarily good state of preservation. The entrance is via a long, low passageway, lined with stone. At first, it seems remarkable only because the walls which still stand are in such good condition. Then you come to a recess where a great stone slab can be moved across as a door, and beyond that the passage is lined by truly massive stones, the largest being 5.4 metres (18 feet) long, 1.2 metres (4 feet) high, and 18 centimetres (7 inches) thick. Bent double, I made my way down this avenue of stone and then stood up in the main chamber, a masterpiece that no skilled mason would be ashamed to own as his work. The walls are composed of carefully prepared stone blocks, set and aligned with great precision up to a height of 1.5 metres (5 feet), after which each successive layer of stone has a slight overlap, so that the walls begin to converge to form a dome or corbelled ceiling. There are also small side chambers, which once held the bones of the dead. If ever there was a place where the popular, comic-book notion of Stone Age man as a club-swinging ignoramus could be dispelled then this is the place. One is at once struck by both the quality of the work and the organization that must have been needed to build such a tomb, in which the individual stones can weigh as much as 3 tonnes. And, as if that were not enough, we find that the whole structure has been placed with such accuracy that, at the winter solstice, the setting sun shines straight down the entrance passage to light the back wall.

Those who were buried in Maes Howe were sent on their way to the next world with their riches still around them, but we can no longer tell what form that treasure took. The tomb was robbed, and the robbers left their own mementoes in the form of carved and scratched graffiti –

The faint marks scratched on the stone wall inside Maes Howe are runes, graffiti left by Vikings who robbed the tomb in the twelfth century. The Norsemen's inscriptions tell of the great treasure they found here.

and those marks are almost as interesting as the tomb itself. The writing is in the form of runes, the script of the Vikings. Suddenly we find ourselves jumping forward in time to the twelfth century AD. There are twenty-four inscriptions in all, some of the commonplace variety you find today – the Kilroy was here, I love Ethel kind – but others offer more tantalizing fragments of a story. These were intended as a record of events, and one message tells us that 'these runes that man cut who is most skilled in rune-craft'. They tell of Earl Harold and his men sheltering here during a great snow storm and, most tantalizing of all, they tell of a treasure they found here and carried away. The plunderers spent three nights removing their hoard from the tomb, but there is absolutely no indication whatsoever as to what form that treasure took. What we do have, however, in these few scratched notes is a picture of Viking life which seems to fit comfortably with our notion of these men, as marauders sweeping down in their dragon-prowed longships to pillage defenceless communities. In the course of this walk, a rather different picture was to emerge.

Leaving Maes Howe for the outside world, I walked down to the old Tormiston water mill which, in other circumstances, one might have seen as an historic feature, but which now seemed quite brashly modern, an impression greatly enhanced by the fact that it is now one of the regular stopping places for tourist coaches. Such intrusions rarely disturb the peace of Orkney, and soon the Neolithic world was again making a dramatic impact on the landscape, though the latter scarcely needed any historic emphasis to make it appealing. Two great sheets of water meet here, the lochs Stenness and Harray. They are now a mecca for fishermen who can be seen standing, apparently motionless, while rippling wavelets slap round their waders or they sit, equally still, in boats out on the loch. The true native inhabitants, however, are the birds, and Harray was home to a huge flock of swans that covered one end of the loch like a carpet of white lilies. This meeting place of the waters must have had some special significance for the people who lived here some 4000 and more years ago, for it is the focal point for a whole group of monuments. The first indication of what was to come was a single stone, standing at the crossing where the road turned north towards the lochs, and this stone links back with Maes Howe. It can be no accident that it stands in a direct line with the entrance passageway of the cairn.

At the end of the promontory, which marks the meeting point of the two lochs, stands an impressive group of stones, the remnants of the Ring of Stenness. This is what archaeologists call a henge monument. When laymen think of henges, they tend to think of circles of standing

The few remaining standing stones of the Ring of Stenness. The horizontal stone in the centre of the ring was found to have traces of charcoal, suggesting it was once used as an altar.

stones, such as Stonehenge, but even Stonehenge itself was stoneless when first built, for the characteristics of this kind of monument are a circular – very occasionally oval – bank with a ditch inside it and one or more entrances. It was this type of henge we saw at Dorchester. Stones are a common, but not essential, accompaniment to a henge. Here, four of the original twelve stones still stand, impressive even in this depleted form. At the centre is what appears to be a small hearth, formed by horizontal stones. Excavation and analysis showed charcoal and pottery sherds, and it does not seem too fanciful to think of this hearth as a form of altar, a centrepiece for the ritual of the stones.

We are still by no means at the end of this part of the story. A bridge now crosses to the northern promontory, and by it stands another great monolith, the Watch Stone, which once had an even grander companion, the Odin Stone. How these stones related to the Stenness henge is not known, but now they led me on to the literally monumentally impressive Ring of Brodgar. Here the bank and ditch, with two opposing causeway entrances, are very prominent features. Yet they are still only pale shadows of their former selves, for excavation has shown that the ditch was once up to 9 metres (30 feet) wide and over 3 metres (10 feet) deep, and cut down into the bedrock. This gives the entrance causeways real significance, for they would once have been the only means of access to the central area of the henge. Nearly half of the stones of what was once a sixty-stone ring still stand so that the ring, in its setting of rough moorland and lakes, still retains much of its austere grandeur. It is easy to see Maes Howe for what it is, a giant tomb, but

The Ring of Brodgar. This great henge monument once had a ring of sixty stones, nearly half of which are still standing today.

what can one possibly make of the Ring of Brodgar? Professor Alexander Thom, who has spent much of his professional life studying this and similar monuments sees them as vast astronomical calculators, laid out in special relation to surrounding landmarks so that events, such as eclipses, could be forecast. It is an attractive theory for many people who like to think of the ancients as possessing special secrets which sadly have been lost, but there is nothing in what we know of the life of the period to suggest anything like that degree of sophistication. Life seems, by modern standards, to have been hard and depressingly short. Nevertheless, even the most hardened cynics sense some curious and unidentifiable aura here. It may be no more than a natural reaction to the great age and sheer scale of the ring. This reaction is intensified by the open setting, where the stones are seen against the ever-changing patterns of the Orkney sky. I have visited this ring on days when black clouds tinged with purple glowered over the stones, which then seemed themselves touched by some sinister inner light, and I have been here when the sun picked out the rich gold of the sandstones and splashed it with the orange of lichens. But if the modern visitor is moved by the ring, then he or she is only following in a long tradition.

As the age of stone, the Neolithic age, gradually gave way to the Bronze Age, so customs changed. The familiar shapes of barrows began to appear on the Orkney skyline – and they concentrated around the older sites of ritual and magic, the henges. They reach right up to the very edge of the ring and can be seen silhouetted on the nearby hillside.

Other visitors came later and left their marks and, once again, one can find Viking runes, this time carved into the stones. There are places where history seems to come in neatly labelled segments but this is seldom so in Orkney. Already I was beginning to feel not so much that I was stepping into the distant past, but that I was merely sampling an episode in a continuous story, where place was of greater importance than time.

After this great flurry of ancient monuments, the next section of the walk at least gave me a chance to draw breath and look at the Orkney scene in a rather more general way. Those who think of Scotland and walking tend to think of the Highlands, of deep lochs and high hills with heather-covered slopes, perhaps dotted by tall pines and leading up to a craggy crown. There is none of that in Orkney. There was no clearly defined edge to the waters of Loch Harray, for the ground simply slides gently under the waves and, out on the horizon, the low hills appear as no more than a dark smudge between water and sky. Wherever I looked, the land was in use, a complex patchwork of small fields marked off by stone walls and occasionally, and somewhat unusually to my eyes, stone fences – flat, upright stones set in rows and strung with wire. It only came as a surprise because, being English, I have a simple pattern in my mind which says that walls are stone or brick, fences wood. But as I looked around the landscape I became aware of the missing feature: trees. The absence of trees is easily explained for Orkney is seldom

The cliffs show the typical stratification of the rock into shallow layers which, on the surface, splinter and crack to form stone slabs which are easily removed. Such slabs formed the basic building material of such great monuments as Maes Howe.

calm and the strong winds slide over the low hills carrying salt water on their breath. Trees can only be grown in the most sheltered of spots, and, once they raise their heads above the parapet, they are blasted by the wind and simply cease to grow. In such a landscape, stone is often called on to take over roles usually filled by timber; in Orkney the Stone Age has never really ended. The older houses that begin to appear soon confirm this view, with their low stone walls and roofs composed of big stone 'tiles', traditionally covered by turf for added insulation and to fill in the gaps. It might seem that this treeless landscape of low hills and endless small fields would be dull, but Orkney has its own special ingredient that turns these seemingly dreary elements into magnificent visual effects, and that is the constantly changing light. In the pure air of the islands, the light has a great clarity and the constant winds ensure that the sky is never still. The busy movements overhead are reflected in constantly shifting patterns of shade and colour on the land. No-one can ever claim to have seen all of Orkney in all its moods, for Orkney is never still.

One can easily become mesmerized by the wide view of the landscape and its ever changing light show, but there was still much to see somewhat closer at hand. As I left the shores of Harray to take the road along the northern edge of the Loch of Stenness, I came across a stony mound marked on the map as the remains of Stack Rue Broch, though the remains themselves gave nothing away. Other broch sites were to prove considerably more revealing. At the end of the loch was another mill building, similar to that at Tormiston. These Orkney mills seem to appear with remarkable frequency and are considerably larger than one would expect to find serving similar scattered communities in England. The difference in size does not, however, indicate a busier mill, but a different type of mill reflecting the special needs of the islands. The predominant crop is barley which requires rather different processing techniques from those used for the wheat grown further south. Once again, all this was to be made clearer further along the walk.

Now I took the road towards the coast which passes through one of the few wild areas in this part of the island, a region of rough moorland and peaty burns which, at best, can provide rough grazing for sheep. The coast itself presented a somewhat bleakly unattractive face at first, for I arrived at the crumbling remains of a World War 2 military installation. But this was only the briefest of interruptions to what was otherwise to prove a quite superb coastline. From the clifftop, I could look south to Hoy where the Old Man's head could be seen peering above the hump of the land. But it was the cliffs themselves that were to provide the key to the nature of many of the things I had already seen,

The narrow, twisting entrance to one of the huts at Skara Brae, designed to keep out the wind that whistled across the nearby Atlantic Ocean.

for under my feet was a natural, rocky pavement of huge flagstones. The local sandstone comes in layers, which then split to form square and oblong blocks, an ideal building material ready shaped by the weather. It was this natural preparation of the stone that eased the work for the builders of Maes Howe, and which provides such items as roofing materials for modern times. The stones are there to be picked up for fence posts or taken away for more substantial buildings. But the forces that have created this shattered pavement are also eating steadily into the cliffs. Down at the water's edge, caves form, and the force of water driving into the undercut caves sends shock waves shivering up through the rock like a pneumatic drill. The forces create holes that reach from sea to clifftop. In time, caves develop into arches and, as the arches break, so sections of cliff become detached from the mainland as separate rock stacks.

I set off to walk northwards along the cliff with an accompanying squadron of arctic terns, who apparently resented my presence for they kept swooping down aiming straight at my head and then wheeling away at the very last moment. I walked hurriedly away from the aggrieved birds only to find a huge, heavy shouldered bull grazing in the next field, but as he had his harem of cows in attendance and seemed quite uninterested in the passerby, I walked on round a deep inlet. Across the water I could see my next objective, the stump of a hollow, circular tower, the Broch of Borwick. One of the pleasing features of this walk was that I was constantly getting trailers for coming attractions. This particular broch was at least recognizable as a massive stone tower, but its lifespan is limited. The sea's steady encroachment is eating away the cliff on which it stands and its eventual total ruin seems inevitable. But, as with the mill, I knew that I had only to be patient and, in time, I would find a substantial and fully excavated broch that I could explore in more detail.

Looking from the inside of one of the huts towards the low, narrow entrance. It is not known what system was used for roofing the huts.

The wind had been rising steadily throughout the day and now the waves were being whipped into a white, creamy topping as I made my way round to the Bay of Skaill. The scene kept changing with extraordinary rapidity as the clouds swept by: at times, the sea seemed a leaden mass, rolling sullenly to a drab shore; the next, the sun transformed the water to a brilliant turquoise and the sand to a gleaming white, so that one could have been staring down on a tropical beach. The effect was somewhat spoiled when I reached the beach itself for the wind sent invisible particles of sand stinging into my face. But all this had a direct bearing on my immediate destination, for it was this shifting sand, blown on the wind, that was the key to the astonishing site I was about to see, Skara Brae.

In the middle of the last century, a violent storm ripped into the dunes at the head of the bay, and as the sand cleared, it revealed an almost perfectly preserved Neolithic village, dating back more than 4000 years. It seems from all the available evidence that it was abandoned as suddenly as it was uncovered, suggesting that what one storm uncovered another, in the third millennium BC, had covered, forcing the people from their homes. It is an extraordinary spot, for we not only see a complete, small village, but we see it in the sort of intimate detail that one would be delighted to find when walking into an undisturbed Victorian farmhouse. The first impression I had was of a sculpted landscape of convoluted shapes, of a system of grassy mounds joined by stone-lined passageways, like a whole group of Maes Howes in miniature. In fact, this is a rather more complex group of buildings than might at first appear. A village existed here somewhere around 3200 BC, and the present village was built over it two centuries or so later. We do at least know just how that was done. The old village had its midden, the decaying debris of village life, and this was piled up by the new builders and allowed to decompose and consolidate, like some giant compost heap. The village was then inserted into the midden itself. Spaces were hollowed out, stone walls built, and entrances constructed as long, narrow, twisted passageways. The nature of the roof is uncertain, but might have been turf set over rafters of bone or driftwood. It might seem a somewhat unsavoury way of life to us today but it had many advantages. The midden not only protected the houses, but generated heat of its own so that, if life was a touch aromatic, you were at least warm, cosy, and well protected from the wind. It is not the overall design that strikes the visitor, however, but the details, for the furnishings of the houses have also been preserved. Inside the living area there are beds and cupboards, cooking hearths, and what can only be described as Welsh dressers. There are even small cubicles attached to the drainage system, which might well have been Neolithic lavatories. And everything is made in stone, even the dresser. The box beds are made out of slabs of stone, and would once have been filled with moss and bracken, making them perfectly comfortable.

There are seven of these houses in all, and one other building which appears to have been a workshop, where stone and flint tools were fashioned, and the remains of a hearth suggest that the stone may have been heated to make it more workable. This is a village which offered comfort to the dwellers, who lived much as people on Orkney have always lived. They kept farm animals, grew crops, notably a form of barley known as bere, and fished. It appears to have been an egalitarian society and a peaceful one, for Skara Brae was occupied with no evidence of trouble for 500 years. For those who had previously only known of Neolithic man from a few artefacts and the great, yet mysterious, tombs and monuments, Skara Brae suddenly brings him to us with a fresh intimacy. The brutish figure of legend disappears in favour of a community of hard-working farmers and fishers, not so very different from the crofters of more recent times.

I returned to Skara Brae the next morning to continue my walk northwards along the coast, past the ruins of yet another water mill. The land now began to rise gently but steadily until it presented a jagged face of rock to the sea. The cultivated land and the fields of grazing sheep and cattle stretch almost to the water's edge, leaving the narrowest of corridors as a footpath. And all the time, I was climbing and the cliffs were getting taller, their ledges home to a variety of seabirds, including one head-cocking puffin. A few gulls rode the wind above the isolated stack, the Spord. Just beyond Outshore Point, another mound blipped the straight line of the horizon, not a mound you could 'read' like the barrows or the chambered cairns, but more a nondescript pile without any great regularity. The map labels it 'burnt mound' and it represents just one of many such mounds which, in fact, consist of heaps of stones, each of which shows the signs of scorching. This time, alas, the walk was not going to provide an opportunity for closer inspection but I made a separate journey down to the Liddle burnt mound on South Ronaldsay. Excavation has revealed the walls of a simple Bronze Age hut beside the pile of stones. Water was channelled into the hut from a nearby spring, but the only other features on the inside are a stone trough and a hearth. We now know exactly what the burnt mounds are. The trough was filled with water, the stones heated on the hearth and then immersed in the water to bring it to the boil. This was, in short, a cookhouse, where big joints of meat could be boiled. If this seems a somewhat fanciful explanation, then it has to be said that this same cooking technique was

The building technique used for this simple fisherman's hut is basically the same as that used some 5000 years earlier at Skara Brae. The stone for building is there on the beach, ready for use.

recorded as still being in use in the Hebrides as recently as the eigthteenth century.

Beyond this point, the sea has carved out a deep cleft and, as I approached it, I thought for a moment that I was coming on a fresh set of prehistoric mounds to tease the imagination. It was only when I was quite close that I found them to be the turf-covered roofs of a huddle of fishing huts. And for a moment, it was as if I was back at Skara Brae, for here was the same dry stone walling, the same use of sandstone slabs, the same need to crouch low to the ground for protection from the wind. The two sets of buildings were separated by some 4000 years, yet they used identical materials in identical ways. But I was about to be brought firmly back to the twentieth century. The land dropped down to sea level and then climbed steadily to Marwick Head, topped by a prominent stone tower, the Kitchener memorial. Lord Kitchener set sail from Scapa Flow for Russia on 5 June 1916 on the cruiser *Hampshire*. The ship was about a mile (1.6 km) off Marwick Head when she hit a mine and sank. There were twelve survivors, but Kitchener was not among them. The tragedy caused a deal of resentment among the locals, for the top brass were more concerned with wartime security than rescue and refused all help from the experienced lifeboat men of Orkney. Sailors were left to make their way, if they could, from the sea up the fierce cliffs. Many who might have made it to safety with a little help were drowned, or battered to death against the rocks.

The dramatic cliffs at Marwick Head. The tower is the Kitchener Memorial which commemorates the death of Lord Kitchener in 1916 when the cruiser Hampshire *on which he was travelling hit a mine a mile (1.6 km) off shore.*

Today, the area is a nature reserve, for the cliffs are home to a huge, raucous colony of seabirds. You smell them before you see them, for the stench of ammonia comes rushing in with the wind from the sea. Marwick Head is one great, overcrowded slum, with birds jostling, shoving, and arguing on every available ledge. Literally tens of thousands of guillemots and kittiwakes have their homes here, and some at least seemed to be wishing they were somewhere else as a gale blew across the sea towards them. I dropped down on to a broad, stone ledge for a close look at this vertical city and found a cowering kittiwake. Startled, it attempted to take off but was caught by the wind and tumbled backwards until it hit an updraught that sent it soaring like a lift in a skyscraper. He was luckier than some of his compatriots for I found many a dead seabird on the walk that morning. Archaelogical evidence shows that once these birds were caught and eaten, while the rarer specimens were selected as food for the dead in the chambered cairns.

The winds began to moderate as I came down towards Birsay Bay. Once this was the centre of Orkney life, where the earls of Orkney had their palace. One automatically thinks of Orkney as being part of the British Isles and, though the union of Scotland and England is of comparatively recent date, at least one thinks of these islands as owing allegiance to the king in Edinburgh. In fact, the earls of Orkney received their titles from Scandinavia, and these islands did not officially become

The causeway which, at low tide, gives access to the Brough of Birsay. The oblong marks on the grassy slope represent the foundations of the buildings that make up the Viking village.

Scottish until almost the end of the fifteenth century. You can catch something of the Norse ancestry in the speech of the Orcadians. For if you stop listening to the actual words and concentrate on the intonation, then you could easily believe yourself to be in Sweden.

The Palace, a somewhat gaunt ruin which even in its heyday could hardly have been very cheery, actually dates from the Scottish period, having been built in the sixteenth century. But tradition has it that the village of Birsay stands on the site of an earlier Norse palace and cathedral. That is open to debate, but indisputable evidence of Norse settlement lies just a short way off. Just across from the point of Buckquoy lies an island, the Brough of Birsay, which can be reached by a causeway for a period of three hours on either side of low tide. I walked across while the Orkney weather performed one of its magic tricks. To one side the sea was a gun-metal grey, touched with tarnished silver on the wavetops: to the other side it was a deep ultramarine and I could look down on to swirls of waving seaweed in the calm, deep pools.

The Brough of Birsay offers evidence of occupation by two quite different groups of people. The first were the Picts, somewhat shadowy figures in history. Their name Picti means 'Painted Ones' and their kingdom stretched all over northern Scotland until they united with the Scots in the ninth century AD. They are known principally from the carved symbol stones they left behind, one of the finest of which was

This carved stone, showing three warriors, an eagle, and geometric designs, stands as evidence of the Picts who lived on Birsay until the Vikings came in the ninth century.

found here. It shows three spear-carrying warriors, dressed in long tunics, with an eagle, an unidentifiable beast, a crescent and decorated disc. The original has gone to the Royal Museum of Scotland, but a replica of the vertical stone stands on the site. Apart from a covered well, almost nothing else remains of the Pictish settlement, for at some time in the ninth century, a new settlement was established by Vikings.

I had already met the piratical Vikings of popular romance, the treasure seekers, the tomb robbers of Maes Howe, but here was a very different story. This was a prosperous village, a settled community with a fine Christian church at its centre. If all that sounds rather tame, the story of the conversion of Orkney does have the true Viking touch. The Orkneyinga Saga tells how Olaf Trygvasson had a profitable few years of looting and pillage around the British coast in the tenth century, but was then baptized in the Scillies. He sailed for Orkney with five ships and a true missionary zeal. He met Earl Sigurd and converted him to the faith by offering a simple choice between conversion or death. The earl, not surprisingly, embraced Christianity and promised that the rest of the Norse people would follow his example.

The church on Brough of Birsay is Romanesque in style, quite small but elaborate with a semicircular apse and the foundations of a square

The remains of a typical Viking long house with its central hearth. The thick walls were faced with stone, both inside and out, the space between being packed with turf and soil.

The rocky shore and shattered cliffs of Orkney provide a source of ready made building materials.

The Wye Valley.

tower. All around it are the foundations of the Norse houses, set out in stone – like plans on a drawing board. They cover a variety of different periods, from Pictish to Norse, but it is the Norse longhouses that are easiest to see. The shape is a simple rectangle, with door openings in the thick walls: stone on the outside, a core of turf, and stone inner walls. A central hearth can also be seen. The houses are large, up to 18 metres (60 feet) long, but I was most struck by their basic simplicity, no more complex in essence than the houses across the water at Skara Brae. This was an important centre of Norse life in the islands, approached by a grand ceremonial entrance, a paved way that once sloped down to the shore, but now stops in mid-air, as erosion has eaten away the ground beneath it. Later, this tiny settlement was to be home to a monastery, the remains of which can be seen alongside the church and its graveyard. It all seems far removed from longships and warriors in horned helmets.

Excavation was still in progress on the Brough of Birsay as I left to retrace my steps back across the causeway to head off towards the Loch of Boardhouse, where I was to fill in the details of one of the other Orkney stories that had begun the previous day. Here is the last working water mill on the island, and it really is a working mill and not merely a museum piece. Again, this is a large building with an overshot wheel thrashing round outside. This is one of the more efficient varieties of water wheel. The commonest is the undershot, which sits in the middle of its mill stream and is turned by the force of water hitting the paddles round the rim. With the overshot wheel, the water arrives in a trough, set at a high level above the wheel. The water then falls into 'buckets' set round the edge of the wheel. As each bucket is filled in turn, so gravity carries it downwards until the turn of the wheel empties it and the cycle starts again. Efficiency, however, has to be paid for in terms of greater structural work to bring the water to the mill.

Once inside the mill, I found out why it is so large. Before the grain is ground, it has to be dried in a kiln, a process not needed in the flour mills of England. Here they make oatmeal, peasemeal, made from roasted field peas, and beremeal, made from bere, the ancient form of barley grown by the people of Skara Brae. There is probably little difference in the processes other than that, in prehistoric times, the grinding would have been done by hand. Here there are three pairs of stones and an assortment of elevators and cleaning machinery, all powered by water. Little has changed here since the mill was built in 1873. To add a footnote, I can say that I did use the beremeal to make traditional beremeal bannocks. The flavour was far stronger than one gets with modern meals and flours but not greatly to my liking.

The soaring Gothic arches of Tintern Abbey.

The Dounby click mill. This type of mill was brought to Orkney from Scandinavia. The large opening at the base of the mill contains the horizontal water wheel which was turned directly by the stream. The water course was dry when this photograph was taken.

The road runs along the north side of Boardhouse Loch, squeezing into a narrow strip of land between the water and Kirbuster Hill. It is a very typical Orkney scene of intensive land use. The farms and small-holdings come at regular intervals, each with its patchwork of tiny fields, some under grass, some set with crops. Drains have been cut from the hill to improve the land, but the hill itself has proved too rough and boggy even for a determined Orcadian to plough. At Kirbuster itself, a truncated cone at the end of a farm building caught my eye. It was easily identifiable as a grain kiln, and when I got closer I found a farm only recently opened to the public as a museum. I stopped to look round and was very glad indeed that I did, for it added yet another link into the chain connecting modern Orkney to the Orkney of prehistory. It was a simple stone building with equally simple stone outhouses, but what made it remarkable was the interior. The principal room had a central hearth, where a cauldron was suspended over a fire of glowing peat and above which fish were hung from a beam to be dried and smoked. Furniture was plain and included the traditional Orkney chair with its high wicker back. The design reflects the shortage of timber in the islands, a lack which appeared even more apparent when I looked at the sleeping arrangements. The box bed was formed from stone flags, precisely as it was at Skara Brae. What astonished me more than anything was that this house and its furnishings are just as they were when it was occupied as recently as the 1970s.

Gradually, as I walked on westwards, I found the fields diminishing and a new landscape of hill and moorland taking over, as the strip of cultivated land became ever narrower. The soggy valley bottom of Durka Dale has now few uses, but its burn was once put to good use, for there are more burnt mounds down by the water. My eventual destination was Evie, but I made a short detour down the Dounby road to visit the Dounby Click Mill. I took a path that led across to a group of buildings that stood on the edge of a wild area of undulating moor through which the soil showed blackly and dark, peaty streams ran. Beside one of these stood the mill, no grand building this time but a turf-roofed stone building no bigger than one of the fishermen's huts on the coast. Yet it is, in its way, a vital part of the Orkney story for it forms another link back to the Norsemen.

The watermill was well known in ancient times, and almost all the mills we see in Britain are, like Boardhouse Mill, descendants from a type first introduced by the Romans. In these a vertical wheel turns on a horizontal axis. There was, however, a second variety that was used in ancient Greece and depended on fast mountain streams to turn the wheel. From Greece it travelled through the Baltic States and up into Scandinavia where it became very popular. The Scandinavians, in turn, brought it to Britain. The Dounby mill is one of the few survivors of that tradition. It differs from the more familiar watermill in that there is no wheel as such, just a vertical shaft with paddles at one end that dip down directly into the fast stream. It was very simple to build for no gears were needed as the stones could simply be set on top of the shaft to be turned directly by the spinning paddles below. All that the miller now needed was a hopper above the stones to hold the grain and a box below to catch the flour or meal. Nothing could be simpler. It represents the positive side of the Norse settlement of Orkney, for mills such as this could take over from the drudgery of hand-grinding using the quern.

The most direct route to Evie was straight across the moor but a few tentative steps on the soft, squelchy peat was enough to convince me that the road offered a more attractive alternative. One tends to think of these great peat bogs as being a permanent feature of the landscape, yet on Orkney they are really of quite recent origin. In Neolithic times they were still forming out of the rotting vegetation of an earlier age, so that the inhabitants of Skara Brae would have had some difficulty acquiring fuel. The likeliest source would have been the dried dung of their animals, supplemented by any drift wood the seas carried to the shore. Today, peat is, as it has been for generations, cut for fuel and the deep peat trenches can be seen all over the dark heathland. But if a continuous tradition had seemed to be the keynote for Orkney, the island still had one surprise to spring to show that the Orcadians could at times appear in the forefront of research. Up to the north on Burgar Hill is what looks like a giant aeroplane propeller on a tall mast. It is, in fact, a windmill that turns a generator which feeds electricity into the local grid.

I reached the coast by the white Sands of Evie, opposite the island of Rousay. The Eynhallow Sound with its small island in the middle looked a trifle ruffled, while streamers of white foam showed where the tide was ripping through the narrows. But it had turned into a lovely day, flotillas of white clouds sailed above the blue sea and the sun shone on a rich green turf and sparkling sands. Out on the headland I could see a pile of stones rising up, but it was not until I reached the point itself that the indistinct shape resolved itself into the last, but not the least significant, of my Orkney sites. I had travelled through Neolithic times to the Bronze Age and then leapt forward to the Pictish kingdom and the Norse men. Now it was time to fill in the gap and round off the walk at the Iron Age Broch of Gurness.

To reach the broch itself I first had to cross a series of encircling ditches and earth ramparts, though to describe them as 'encircling' is no longer strictly true, for the sea has nibbled away and devoured almost half the ring. But these are merely preludes to the main theme, the remains of the broch itself. It appears now as a ruined circular tower, rising at its highest point about 3 metres (10 feet) above ground level, though it seems likely from looking at similar structures on Shetland, that it might originally have been as much as four times that height. It surrounds a courtyard just over 9 metres (30 feet) in diameter. Now it is no easy task to build a stone tower of such a size to such a height, and the job becomes even more difficult when you have no timber for scaffolding. The tower has, in fact, two stony skins with a gap between. The builders were able to raise their walls to a suitable height and then cross the gap with stone slabs to form a gallery from which they could begin building upwards once again. On completion, the space between the walls became a complex of corridors, staircases, and even small cells.

Down in the courtyard, the floor is divided into two areas, the larger having a cooking tank similar to that found at burnt mounds, a large hearth, and a number of compartments defined by stone slabs. There is also a deep well reached by a flight of stone steps. Another flight of steps leads upwards to the first-floor landing. From here I could see how the broch formed the centrepiece of a cluster of small buildings radiating outwards and hugging its walls. The first impression is that the broch was undoubtedly a defended settlement – that much is obvious, and indeed the defences are quite formidable. But quite how the the whole system worked is not so clear. Families lived in the 'village' outside the

tower walls, but was the broch itself permanently occupied or was it kept in readiness as a place of retreat when the community was under attack? Answers are not easy to come by and the whole affair is made more complicated because the broch's usefulness extended well beyond the age in which it was built. The Vikings found the great tower much to their liking, and the outline of a longhouse can be seen inside the complex. The grave of a Viking lady was also discovered here.

It is not surprising that the Vikings adapted the brochs: after all, they knew the value of defence against marauders from the sea, being notably successful marauders themselves. But should we think of the broch as the stronghold of a warlike people, or as a safe shelter established by people who only wanted to be left in peace? I spotted the stone from a rotary quern among the ruins of the outer houses, but excavations resulted in some less attractive discoveries. A group of bronze rings were found – the macabre touch being that they were attached to fingers on severed hands casually dropped into the kitchen midden.

The brochs were, by any standards, massive achievements, but now

The Iron Age Broch of Gurness. This great tower was built with a double wall: the staircase in the foreground actually passes up between the two layers. Small houses cluster round the outside of the fortress.

at the end of my journey it was not the scale of the enterprise which struck me – after all why should I be astonished by the skill and ingenuity of Iron Age builders when I had already seen what the Stone Age had achieved at Maes Howe? I was most impressed by the details of domestic life on show, and how one was looking at a system which, in its essentials, was as much like the far earlier settlement of Skara Brae as it was the farmhouse at Kirbuster. For thousands of years, it seems, people have taken the flagstones of Orkney, so thoughtfully provided by nature, and have come up with solutions to the problems of building that have hardly changed through the millennia. This is, of course, a simplification of a complex story, based on just one walk on just a part of one island. Across the water I could see Rousay, and just make out the ruins of another broch and the mound of chambered cairns, while a glance at my map provided the site of a Norse Hall. Last time I had come to Orkney I had told myself that I had to return. All I could do now was say the same thing all over again.

The extraordinary Neolithic village of Skara Brae, which was covered by a sandstorm in the third millennium BC and only rediscovered when another storm blew away the sand in the nineteenth century.

CASTLES OF THE WYE

Goodrich to Chepstow, 30 miles (48 km), OS maps 162,172.

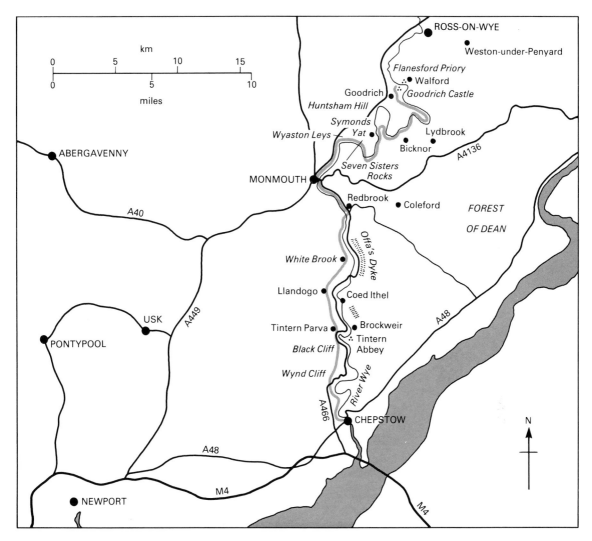

Apart from a few minor deviations, the route followed was that of the waymarked Wye Valley Walk between Goodrich and Chepstow. The name might suggest a gentle stroll along a river bank, but a glance at the map soon shows that the line of the walk goes straight across several of those ominous sections where the contour lines crowd together. The walk, in fact, turned out to be at least partly that undemanding waterside ramble, but the other part consisted of slogs up to the rim of the valley, where the effort of getting up was at least rewarded by spectacular views. A closer look at the map also showed that much of the route lay

The valley of the Wye is now noted for its beauty, but, in previous centuries, it was thought of principally as a frontier. The fast-flowing river and steep, densely forested bank forming an all-but-impenetrable barrier.

through woodland. Now, the woods of summer may look superb, with faint light drilling through leaves that shade from a translucent pallor where they catch the sun to a dense, close-packed green that darkens to shadows of indigo. The sound of the summer woodland is, however, all too often that of the incessant murmur of insects which seem to find the salty sweat of perspiring humans an irresistible lure. Summer has a further disadvantage: the density of the leaves which adds so much to the beauty of the scene, also serves to obscure the view. As the main object of the walk was to view human history, not natural history, I opted for a walk in March.

March is a month that hovers indecisively between winter and spring. It seemed, in the days before I had hoped to start the walk, that it had opted firmly for winter. Snow swept the country, carried on the back of a harsh east wind. It seemed unlikely that I should be able to reach the Wye, let alone walk it. Then, quite suddenly, March decided that it had had enough: the wind crept away from the east, the leaden clouds lifted, and I was presented with the very best weather a walker could hope to enjoy. The sky was clear and clean, a finest blue porcelain with a few white chips of clouds. The temperature was perfect: a little chilly for standing around, but just right for exercise. The omens seemed favourable, and my chosen starting point produced instant indications of some of the themes that were to predominate throughout the walk.

The beginning was at Goodrich Castle but, before looking at the castle itself, it is as well to see just why it exists at all. The reasons soon pile in, starting with perhaps the most obvious and important of all; this is border country. Today, borders are neatly drawn lines on accurate maps, but in an earlier age a border represented at best an agreed demarcation, but often meant nothing more than a line that could be defended. The river heading south from Goodrich forms just such a defensible barrier, running in a narrow valley, but to the north, it opens out into a wide flood plain, a somewhat less daunting obstacle. Here, one can see at once, natural defences are simply not going to be enough. Those who would control such an area need a centre of control. A commanding hilltop is the obvious answer, but which of many hills would you select? Here geography supplies the answer.

If you look at the river immediately north of the castle you can see it widen and stretch to become sluggish and reedy. This has all the appearance of a fordable point, and there is an even more significant

The massive stone walls of Goodrich Castle are set on the natural rock and rise high above the moat. In the foreground are the foundations of the castle's stables.

sign on the opposite bank. A minor road runs straight at the river, passes a small wood and then stops; but a path on just the same alignment runs up alongside the castle towards the village of Goodrich. The straightness of the line is significant for this is the track of a Roman road, which linked the centre of Ariconium, near present-day Weston-under-Penyard, to Roman Blestium, modern Monmouth. Why the Romans were interested in the Wye Valley will emerge later in the walk but, for the present, it is enough to see the evidence of an ancient crossing point on the river. And there is still more evidence in the name of the village on the opposite bank, Welford, or as it was originally called, Welshford. The last question – where precisely to build the castle – must have been the easiest of all to decide. The hill was there, falling away steeply down to the river on the north side and protected by a secondary, deep valley to the west.

The early history of this castle has left few marks on the ground, but records show that there was a Godric's Castle here by the beginning of the twelfth century. The Normans had only recently pushed the Welsh away from the west bank of the river, and it would be natural to want to hold on to the lands by protecting such a vital crossing point. The likeliest candidate for the first builder is Godric Mappestone, after which the land passed through a bewildering array of owners in the endless feudings between the Norman lords and the crown. It achieved its greatest hour when it was the seat of the earls of Shrewsbury. Something of those changing fortunes can still be read in the stones of Goodrich Castle.

Seen from a distance, the castle seems all of a piece, a great fortress set high on its rocky base. It soon appeared as I got closer that this sense of completeness and unity of construction is an illusion and that, like most such castles, the centuries have seen many additions and not a few subtractions. But that first approach established the essential character of the place. Whatever else it might have been, it was first and foremost a stronghold and an impressive one at that. As I strolled up the gentle slope towards the castle entrance, I could see that the outer walls were built from the same rich, red sandstone on which the whole structure rests. There would have been no problem in finding building material, for tonnes of rock must have been shifted to form the moat that protects the southern and eastern sides. The entrance itself is heavily guarded. An outer defence, or barbican, stands away from the castle across the moat, surrounded by its very own secondary moat. So anyone entering the castle by the official front door, as it were, had to cross the first moat, pass through the barbican, and then turn to cross a second bridge across the main moat. The approach is a long one, with the bridge being carried on two arches, and part of it being a pivoted drawbridge. Intruders were not encouraged, and the message becomes doubly clear at the gatehouse itself where there are indications of two sets of gates, and slits show where a portcullis could have been dropped. The whole stands under the eyes of the guardhouse, a surprisingly cosy little spot, complete with its own fireplace. All in all, the prospects for a direct attack by the front door look poor, and a would-be attacker inspecting the outer defences might well feel thoroughly daunted.

The massive solidity of the defences at Goodrich can be seen in this view of the heavily fortified sally port – the castle's 'back door'.

A curtain wall rises high and seemingly blank faced above the rocky cutting of the moat, protected at each corner by massive towers. These are perhaps the most striking features of the whole place. They rest on square bases, from which triangular spurs rise up to support the circular towers. These buttresses do more than give support; they also supply a defence against undermining during a siege. This outer shell dates from around 1300 and, to the eye of this twentieth-century visitor, it had an air of total impregnability. I quite simply could not imagine taking such a place without the benefit of modern artillery. Yet, taken it was. When Elizabeth Comyn inherited the castle in 1324, she was forced to cede the rights to Hugh Despencer. Elizabeth's husband, Richard Talbot, laid siege to the fortress in 1326 and it fell. The castle was established as the principal seat of the Talbots, who were created Earls of Shrewsbury in the following century. It was occupied by Royalist forces in the Civil War and, although it was never stormed, the Parliamentarians starved the garrison into submission.

Once inside, the complexity of the castle became rather more obvious. The square keep is clearly an anachronism. Surrounded everywhere by the red sandstone that seemed to glow in the low rays of a wintry sun, it stood grey and stark, a hard-edged limestone bastion, set against the rounded outlines of the towers. It is unmistakeably Norman, built in an age when the owners were uneasy occupants of a hostile land. It is the oldest remaining part of the castle, built in the twelfth century. It seems odd to see limestone used for building when the castle actually sits on sandstone, but the choice would not have been quite so obvious to the original builder, for the castle stands on a geological division between the broad expanse of sandstone and a narrow tongue of Carboniferous limestone that licks up the Wye Valley. Outside the keep, however, sandstone appears as the universal building material. Pacification of the surrounding countryside – or subjection if seen from the viewpoint of the native Welsh – brought a certain relaxation, and style and comfort became as important as protection and defence. On the western side of the courtyard are the great hall and the solar. The most striking feature is a pair of elegant arches that rise the full height of the two-storey solar. Defence, however, was still a concern and a sally-port is heavily protected by doors and a portcullis. The chapel next to the gatehouse provides a striking example of the gradual easing away from the stern necessities of the first castle at Goodrich. The fifteenth-century windows would not look in the least out of place in a peaceful parish church.

To walk round a castle such as Goodrich is to see more than just a building in ruins, it is to get a glimpse of how a community organized its life, to get a notion of its preoccupations. It is, however, easy to look at the bare stone walls and conjure a picture of a grim, dour way of life. But imagine the walls hung with tapestries, rushes to soften the floor, and comfortable furniture, and you begin to imagine a place bustling with life. Castles may have been built as defences against war but, in practice, the inhabitants lived mostly at peace and enjoyed the privileges of prosperity. Details then take on a new significance. When I went to see the stables outside the walls, recognizable by the drainage channel down the middle, I thought of hunting parties rather than armoured knights riding out to combat. The castle may have been tested in war but, for most of its history, it was a place where a community went about its business.

I left the castle and took the road down to the village of Goodrich where the most important building appears to be Ye Olde Hostelrie whose Gothic architecture might well seem appropriate to its setting but which dates back no further than the end of the last century. It was once, however, a quite insignificant sham compared with the much grander Gothic extravagance of Goodrich Court. This was dismantled in 1950, all the stones carefully labelled and then shipped to America for re-erection. It seems an extraordinary compounding of layers of deception to rebuild what was never 'real' in the first place. All that remains of this apparently rather magnificent folly are some wooden panels in the local church. The church, however, can boast some rather more genuine claims to importance. A chalice is a reminder of the days when the Royalist vicar was deprived of his living by the successful Parliamentarians. He became a famous man locally, but the chalice was presented to his even more famous grandson: the persecuted vicar was Thomas Swift and his grandson, Jonathan.

The road runs downhill towards the river and is crossed by a high arched bridge, which I immediately assumed to be a railway bridge, but first impressions were mistaken. It is a road bridge carrying a minor road high above the main road, a most unusual feature to find in a small village. Down by the river stands a fine old barn, which unusually has a cross on the roof, now virtually the only indication that I was looking

These elegant arches rise the full height of the solar at Goodrich Castle, but would seem equally appropriate in some great church or abbey.

The graceful span of the stone bridge across the Wye at Goodrich, built in 1825.

at all that remains of Flanesford Priory, founded in 1346 by Lord Talbot for the Black Friars of the Augustinian order. It was undergoing what is no doubt only the latest of a series of alterations, this time conversion into a house. Here the river is crossed by one of those totally unpretentious stone bridges that are such an attractive feature of the countryside. It is a happy reminder that the nineteenth century gave the world far more than overblown mock medievalism. It was also the century of solid, restrained achievement. The bridge, built in 1825, marks the arrival of the new age of turnpike roads which did so much to improve transport in Britain.

The walk now got properly under way after much of the morning had gone by in happy pottering around the ancient stones of history. Below the bridge, the river sweeps round a wide bend to head almost due east and the walk began in the open fields of the south bank. Openness is seldom a feature of the river scenery for very long and the path soon disappeared into woodland which climbed up an ever steepening hill above the water. It added a further thought about the placing of Goodrich Castle: there was very little need to worry about fortifying this particular stretch of border country, for nature has done a far better job than man could hope to do. The opposite bank provides enough space for a road and a scattering of houses, but here the best that can be managed is a narrow trackway beside the deep, fast-flowing Wye. The land itself dictates where human influence is most clearly seen. Here, on my side of the river, it seemed at first as though the natural world reigned supreme, but land and forest are commodities and, if woodland is to be used productively, it needs to be managed just as any other land that carries a crop needs to be controlled. The significance of the woodland to the whole development of the area seemed to grow in importance with every mile of the walk. But for a time at least I was happy just to be walking a path striped with pale patches of light that fell between the dark shadows of tall trees. Then the woodland petered out and the river swung again, turning right back on itself to flow north-westwards where a few minutes ago it had been running steadily eastwards.

The village of Lydbrook stands across the river, and a low, squat chimney poking out from a cluster of buildings suggested something more than mere domestic use – the remains of a forge perhaps – but it was too far away and the river prevented closer inspection. If I had been able to cross, I would have found an even stronger hint of former use, for the pub close to the water is the Forge Hammer Inn. Closer to hand, however, were reminders of the river's role as a boundary. Welsh Bicknor, with a charming little church, peers across at English Bicknor

The little church at Welsh Bicknor stands beside the Wye, dwarfed by the steep, wooded hillside.

set on a hill on the opposite bank. The path, too, crossed over, not on a road bridge but on what was very obviously a disused railway bridge. It is an entirely utilitarian structure, a wooden bridge carried on iron supports with few claims to grace or beauty. It was, however, perfectly adequate for a minor railway, which is all that this was. The Ross and Monmouth Railway was opened in 1873 between the main Hereford to Gloucester line and Monmouth, and was later extended southward to Chepstow and renamed the Wye Valley Railway. It was, from the first, run by the Great Western Railway and was eventually absorbed into that great empire. So this was very much branch-line territory with little room for frills. Although the bridge itself is an obvious railway feature, it is not quite so immediately clear where the railway ran. In fact it emerged from the hillside where it had just passed through the Bicknor tunnel. And, when you cross the river to what was Lydbrook Junction, the line gets lost again under the modern works of a paper factory.

The few miles of woodland walk might well have seemed little more than a gentle country stroll, but they had added an appreciable number of factors to the valley story, as new transport routes had appeared with traces of old industry and the modern buildings of a still active working life. I set off along the track of the old railway, and my mind began to fill with images of Victorian life. The works were a useful reminder that this was a valley with more to offer than romantic scenery but, nevertheless, I kept thinking of excursion trains hauled by dark-green engines, their tall chimneys crowned with burnished copper. There is an inevitable air of slightly wistful sadness about an old railway line where not even the echo of a steam whistle lingers in the air. It remains recognizable in the landscape, but its function had irretrievably gone. I could not help thinking what a delightful line it must once have been, and what an attractive line it would have made in the world of preserved railways. It was not the only line ruled along the edge of the river. Away to the east, another embankment strode across the skyline. The GWR branch line was keeping company for a while with Offa's Dyke.

Offa's Dyke is a defensive work as remarkable in its way as Hadrian's Wall. Conflict between the regions we now know as England and Wales dates back before the Norman Conquest. In the eighth century, the idea of 'England' was just beginning to emerge as a recognizable concept, already expressed in the name of Bede's famous work *The Ecclesiastical History of the English People*. There was not yet a unified kingdom, but there was a dominant force in the land, Mercia. Offa was the king of Mercia at the end of the eighth century, and a powerful one. The British Celts had been steadily pushed out to the west by the invading Anglo-Saxons, and the latter now needed to consolidate and protect their position. Offa ordered a great defensive work to be built of rampart and ditch that would stretch 149 miles (240 km) from Prestatyn in the north to Sedbury in the south. Its aim was simple. It was a defence against the Welsh – though Offa was by no means averse to sending out raids of his own from behind its protective shelter. It is a remarkable work, and its line is now followed by another long-distance footpath.

Scenery now became a dominant feature, for the walk had now brought me to 'the picturesque Wye'. The scenery, of course, has not changed much in recent centuries – but our appreciation of its beauty is really a very modern phenomenon. In fact, you can almost date it precisely and lay the discovery at the door of one man. The date is 1770, the event the publication of *Observations on the River Wye*, and the man, the author of the book, William Gilpin. It was he who brought in the vogue for the picturesque, with the quite novel idea that people might actually enjoy looking at wild scenery – and he was prepared to tell them how to look. The Wye had all the picturesque elements in plenty: romantic ruins, wooded valleys, and high cliffs. Thanks to Gilpin, a whole new industry came to the Wye valley – tourism. It still thrives today.

The grandeur begins with the Coldwell Rocks, limestone cliffs that rear up above the trees, but the great spectacle lies just ahead. Huntsham Hill seems to lie directly in the river's path, but the river sweeps away off to the north, turns back on itself, and then continues on its way. If you took the shortest possible route round the back of the hill, then you would travel less than half-a-mile (800 metres): the river takes a full 5 miles (8 km) to wind itself round the rocky promontory. My path took a half way point between the two. Those who follow the waymarked route find themselves climbing up the hill and, in wet weather, slithering down again, but the route at least gives a taste of the rocky headland with its magnificent view over the busy, rushing river. And the view is the attraction that has drawn visitors to this spot on the Wye for 200 years – and which has also ensured that the limited space by the river is packed with hotels. The river, however, still divides the flat land, suitable for building, from the crags and cliffs of Symonds Yat that give the visitors their vantage point. So ferries still exist to join the two banks together and the ferry boat inns still thrive, which was good news for this hungry, thirsty walker. But even as one walks the hillside paths, one is made aware that there was once more to this area than just tourism, for collapsed walls, ruined houses and scarred cliffs hidden away in the woodland tell of a busy quarrying trade.

Beyond Symonds Yat is an area with a name that could scarcely fail to set the curiosity bubbling – The Slaughter. Nothing visible on the ground gives even the slightest indication of what happened here, but tradition has it that this was the place where the Roman invaders of Claudius's reign defeated the British under Caractacus. This whole stretch of the river is rich in historical memories but sadly not much of the history appears in visible form. What I got instead was the scenic walk, the Romantic Landscape – very much with capital letters – for the landowners of a century and more ago were enthusiastic devotees of the picturesque. The map shows ancient settlements and hill forts, but they are now lost among the trees and, for compensation, I had the majestic cliffs of the Seven Sister Rocks, where artifice has piled romance upon nature by the addition of pretty grottoes.

The path crossed the river again, this time on a simple suspension bridge and, once across, the signs began to appear to show that I was walking along the edges of a grand estate. Boundaries were marked off by iron railings pierced by ornate gates, and all around the woodland showed signs of coppicing and careful management. Then as the woods began to thin, the buildings began to appear. Estate cottages emblazoned with coats of arms looked out across the river, and cast-iron bollards provided mooring posts for the boats of the salmon fishermen. The area epitomizes one aspect of the nineteenth-century story of the Wye, as a region especially suited to give pleasure to the wealthy. Here they could walk the woods to admire the scenery, or attempt to capture it in water colours, or set out for a day's fly fishing. Eventually, the seat of all this wealth appeared with the mansion of Wyaston Leys.

Now the path was squeezed between the busy main road and the river, but the steady beat of passing traffic did not greatly affect the sense of still being in an essentially rural area. The flattened valley gave wider views of the farms, often boasting quite grand houses. The fields of March were full of grazing sheep and bewildered lambs which, caught by a sharp east wind, must have felt they had sadly mistimed their entries into the world. And so that day's walk ended at the old county town of Monmouth, a town which seemed somehow to sum up the impressions of the day. I had started off thinking in terms of frontiers and Norman knights, and along the way had found myself drawn off to contemplate a whole range of other themes from the tourists in search of the picturesque to the working life of the area. Monmouth brought them all together.

Ideally, to get the perfect historical introduction to Monmouth, you should approach it from the south, but that was not to be the way of it. Instead of history, I was faced with a dual carriageway and popped down the underpass, with its inevitable spray-can graffiti, and popped up again in the town. Perhaps, after all, this is the best way to do it, to see the town as the end product of a period of change rather than as a history lesson set in stone. Times do change and who knows but that historians of the future may find twentieth-century graffiti as revealing about our times as historians of today find the runes at Maes Howe. But my preoccupations were still more with the past than with the present, and memories of the past crowd in quite quickly in Monmouth.

The reason for the town's existence is easily seen, for it sits at the confluence of two rivers, the Wye and the Monnow, and at the heart of an agricultural area. It grew up as a place of strategic importance and as a market, and became one of those towns of modest if not excessive richness which do so much to give Britain its character. On the corner of the main street leading up to the town centre stands the old grammar school, founded in 1614, venerable certainly but again not excessively grand. Beyond that I kept finding buildings of character, but never showy. The centrepiece of the town is Agincourt Square, with its eighteenth-century Shire Hall. Henry V was born in Monmouth in 1387, but he had few associations with the town at any later date. Still, it gives an excuse for a statue of the warrior king – and a very poor statue it is, too. Monmouth is a good place in which to compare the heroes of different ages. Henry has the advantage of having been given his speeches posthumously by Shakespeare, so that everyone now thinks of him as the great and noble leader of his nation. In a later age, kings preferred to conduct their battles by proxy, and the laurels fell to the professional fighters. The town is home to a museum devoted to a man whose fame matched that of Prince Hal, Admiral Horatio Nelson, though the emphasis is at least as firmly placed on his famous romance with Lady Hamilton as on his deeds of war. And what of later ages? War somehow seems less heroic in the days of long-distance bombardment and bombs from the sky, so the names that are recalled are those of the makers of the age – including the engineers. In front of King Henry stands a statue of C S Rolls, who with his partner Royce, founded the famous company that epitomized – and epitomizes – excellence. But take away the heroes and you are left with the comfortable market town, with the usual mixture of buildings from a variety of periods. There is, however, a little more still to be discovered. This was a border town, and the fortification theme with which I began the day again asserted itself.

Near the centre of the town is the castle, or what remains of it. It was important enough in its day as one of the seats of the House of Lancaster but, like many others, it finished up on the losing side in the Civil War and was largely destroyed. But the military presence lingered and the army now inhabits perhaps the finest of all the town buildings, the

Castle House, built in the late seventeenth century. It is certainly the grandest building in town, but not perhaps the most important. In its early days, Monmouth was a walled town and all its approaches were carefully guarded, including the bridge over the Monnow. There, the

The bridge over the Monnow at Monmouth – it was part of the medieval fortification of the town, and later served as a toll house.

old gatehouse – which also served as a toll house – still survives. This is the last remaining fortified bridge of its type anywhere in Britain and, if you see nothing else in Monmouth, you should see this, for it speaks volumes about the precarious past when even the large town had to be prepared for any eventuality.

The next day I set off back across the river to continue my walk down the Wye. Major road systems meet at Monmouth, and I soon found it to be a major rail junction as well. As well as the line from Ross to Chepstow, there were lines from Pontypool and the Forest of Dean. So the river is crossed not just by the now-familiar Wye Valley viaduct, but also by an altogether grander, stone-arched viaduct built in the 1860s for the Coleford, Monmouth, Usk and Pontypool Railway – an impressive name, but it still finished up as a GWR branch line like the rest. After that last touch of urban excitement, the walk took on an altogether calmer and more tranquil mode. The morning could not be described as misty yet a delicate curtain seemed to be suspended between myself and the distant hills. They lacked substance; like the cardboard scenery of a penny plain theatre, they retreated in soft shades of grey. The low rays of the morning sun picked up each ripple on the water and threw it back as a star of light, while across the river shadows moulded the hillside where sheep grazed. On my side of the river, the woodland gradually crept down towards the water and I stopped my romantic musings on the picturesque Wye and concentrated on matters closer at hand. And almost at once I spotted something by the path which brought me right back from rural contemplation to thoughts of a very different sort of world. For there lay a large chunk of purplish-black material that was unmistakable: it was furnace slag. The life of the Wye I had glimpsed briefly when I peered through the trees across the water to Lydbrook had caught up with me again.

The way officially continued along the river past the fringes of the village of Redbrook. But by now my curiosity was aroused, so I turned off up the B4231 to see what might appear. I was not disappointed. Two elements in a complex story turned up at once – a house named 'Old Brewhouse' and extensive remains of old watercourses, controlled by sluices. An even more significant site appeared just up the hill where a most unusual bridge crossed the road, unusual because where most bridges are flat topped, this one had a very pronounced slope. Road bridges are not built like that, nor are conventional railway bridges, so that there was really only one thing that this could be, a tramway incline. In the days before the steam locomotive appeared, industrial areas were served by an early form of railway in which horses did the haulage. In hilly regions, however, tramway engineers used a quite different approach from that of their railway successors. It is a simple matter to unhitch a horse and lead it up or down a hill until the next level section is reached. You can then save on construction by sending your tracks straight down the hill, where gravity will do the work in one direction. All you need then is some mechanism for hauling trucks up the slope. Where there is a one-way traffic of loaded trucks going down and empty trucks going up, the weight of those descending will pull up the empties. Otherwise a simple steam engine or even a waterwheel could provide the power. Here I was looking at the remains of the Monmouth Railway that ran between Monmouth and the Forest of Dean.

Tramways, unlike later railways, were used exclusively for goods traffic, so their existence always implies the presence of industry. At the foot of the incline, I could see a row of workers' cottages and the ruins of a stone building of considerable size. So we have a tramway, water power, copper slag, and a river which turns out to have indications of a considerable wharf area. This is quite enough information to deduce that something important once went on here. I could now add a few extra deductions. The Forest of Dean has iron and coal deposits, but nowhere in the area is there any copper. But the Wye runs down to the Severn and the Severn empties into the Bristol Channel which is the sea route to Cornwall. There were tin and copper mines in Cornwall, but no fuel for smelting. But in the Wye valley there was fuel in plenty. Logic suggests that the copper ore was brought here for smelting, and documents show that Redbrook was a busy little community, where copper was smelted as early as the end of the seventeenth century. Later, a tinplate works was established on the same site. There may be few remains of the works, but they had a long history. In the 1770s, iron sheets were being rolled out using water power; by 1798 steam power had taken over; and in 1944, electricity was doing the job. By then the mills of Redbrook were rolling the thinnest steel plates in the world at just over two-thousandths-of-an-inch (0.05 millimetre) thick. Now the tinplate works have gone. The old brewing premises by the incline occupy part of the site and a transport depot by the river occupies the last of the tinplate buildings, which finally closed in 1962. You can still see an old building which was the manager's house and there is a warehouse near the old wharf.

The river itself is the key to development along the valley. Water provided the only cheap and efficient transport system before the railway age, while water power took on all the heavy work before the arrival of the steam engine. So places like Redbrook developed because there was the right mixture of raw materials and transport. It was better placed than towns along the Severn for, although the latter river offered

The ruins of a paper mill at Whitebrook, one of many that once lined the valley. It was here that paper was made for the old-style, white £5 notes.

better navigation, it lacked the steep sides of the Wye whose tributary streams could power waterwheels. It is difficult now to see it for what it once was, a place of smoking chimneys and clanging metal. The Wye tourists came down here in their pleasure boats, but had little to say about the industrial life of the valley as they floated on their way to the next picturesque encounter.

My walk was set to continue on the Wye Valley Railway again, starting with another of the bridges built to the standard design. I crossed over to the old Boat Inn, another reminder that this was once a trading river. The walk now ran beside the railway for a while and then joined it, the old track bed providing a comfortable way through yet another heavily wooded section. I could see massive moss-covered boulders tumbled among the trees, and some of the huge stones had found their way into the boundary wall. So too had some recognizable mill stones, as another Wye industry laid out its clues for deciphering. There are several indications of quarrying in the woods, and some of the stones went to millwrights who prepared them not for crushing grains but apples. Wye Valley millstones were popular for the cider presses of the West Country.

The first few miles of the day had presented me with a gentle, if far from uneventful ramble but, as the end of the railway section came at the foot of the Whitebrook valley, so the easy walking came to an end. The walk follows the road up the valley and at once it became obvious that the busy brook had been put to work. Beside the farm were the remains

The Wye near Llandogo. The prominent track that runs past the white house is all that remains of the Wye Valley Railway.

of a building and ample indications of the use of water power. More substantial signs soon appeared and it proved well worthwhile walking up the road a little way past the point where the Wye Valley Walk turned off. The signs now were plain: a great complex of buildings, all showing evidence of water power, stood next to some quite grand houses. They were too big to be grain mills, and there were too many of them, yet there were no obvious signs of metalworking in the form of furnaces and hearths. So it was by no means clear just what went on here. Water power can be used for many different processes and what I was in fact looking at was a whole string of paper mills set up along the White Brook in the eighteenth century. They carried on working until near the end of the nineteenth century. They were mostly worked by Bristol-based companies, and some of the paper went into making the old style of white £5 notes.

I lingered a while over the old paper mills, partly out of interest – and partly because the way ahead seemed likely to offer a couple of miles of panting, uphill slog. The first part of the track was more than a simple pathway up the hill. This was an old trading route, carefully protected by stone walls composed of often massive boulders. It seemed at first to be leading nowhere other than to empty hillsides, but then it became clear that the whole area is dotted with small farmsteads, hill farms where the buildings are tightly clustered as protection against the weather. There is a marked contrast between these tight little groupings and the prosperous farms glimpsed on the richer and gentler land on the opposite bank of the river. There was not, however, to be much opportunity to enjoy wide views as the walk headed off into the forest. This was mixed woodland, not the pines on parade that can be found in some parts of the valley. Walking through the woods at the tail end of a spell of wintry weather, the atmosphere seemed more Scandinavian than British. The branches dripped steadily on to the ground, but the tall trunks still carried the white, north-facing stripe of unmelted snow. Near Llandogo a deep cleft carried a cascading stream down towards the Wye, but the forest walk continued along the crest of the hill.

The forest walks have been created for the tourist trade. Benches set in clearings provide an opportunity to sit and enjoy superb views down the valley and broad walkways have been laid out, stretching away from a car park on the Tintern road. There is, however, more here than pleasant strolls in the wood. Immediately below the car park, a sign points down to Coed Ithel, and following it down to a point just above the farm on the main road, I came across one of the few survivors of the first industrial age of the Wye. The site itself is easily recognized as an artificial feature. The most prominent building, set against the hillside, is like a small tower which is narrow at the top, widens out to a point two-thirds of the way down, and then narrows in again. Half of it has crumbled away, leaving the rest in cross-section like a diagram in a text-book. This is, in fact, a blast furnace, where iron ore was heated with charcoal to produce the molten metal. It dates back at least as far as the middle of the seventeenth century, a hundred years before the industrial revolution is said to have begun.

To obtain iron from its ore, the oxygen has to be burnt off using a carbon fuel, but coal, the obvious candidate, has too many impurities. In the eighteenth century, Abraham Darby discovered that coke was ideal for the job but until then charcoal was the only pure fuel available. The Wye Valley again proved to have the right ingredients on hand: iron ore, ample woodland for charcoal making, and the river for transport. A furnace such as this also needed a strong blast of air to raise the temperature of the fire, and you can still see the leat that brought water to the site and the wheelpit where a water wheel turned. The wheel then worked huge bellows that blew air into the furnace at the point where it reached its maximum width. Once you have seen the furnace, other aspects of the area begin to make sense as well: the old tracks through the woods, the managed woodlands themselves, coppiced to provide the right thickness of branch for charcoal making. My curiosity was thoroughly aroused as to what other signs of this ancient industry might appear along the way.

Beyond Coed Ithel, the official walk headed downhill towards Brockweir, but I was drawn towards the road that led down to Tintern

Parva, partly because the map had the magic word 'Inn' at the end of it, and partly because a busy stream flowed down beside the roadway. The instinct that said that a fast-flowing stream through an iron-making area should yield something of interest proved to be sound. Almost at once, signs appeared of artificially created ponds, from which water could be released in a controlled manner to turn a water wheel. The buildings have gone, but it was clear that machinery was once at work in the valley, and there is every reason to believe that the machinery would have been used for working metal. The little valley still teems with water, and one householder has found a most ingenious way of channelling his drainage water down the bank: a cascade of lavatory pans, a kind of porcelain fountain that ran down from the garden to the brook.

The inn was open: pints were consumed in the sun, and the afternoon was free for the exploration of Tintern. This is the most famous, and certainly the most popular, spot in the Wye valley but, before walking on to its most celebrated monument, I backtracked towards the bridge at Brockweir. It is a remarkably graceful, single iron span and, if I had

This silted pond above Tintern was originally created to hold water that could be released to turn a water wheel which in turn powered the huge hammers of the ironworks.

been asked to date it, I would have placed it somewhere in the early part of the last century. I would have been quite wrong, for there was only a ferry across the river at this point until the bridge was completed in 1906. From here, the official walk takes to the railway again but, where before the railway past had been a distant memory, here it became suddenly vivid. Tintern Parva station has been restored, complete with posters announcing such delights as a day excursion to Cardiff Races or a visit to the Royal Military Exhibition, all courtesy of the Great Western Railway. The old signal box has been converted into an information centre and a variety of railway bits and pieces, from signals to distance posts, have been set down beside the track. The railway walk itself, however, comes to an abrupt end at the river bank, where high abutments are all that remain of the viaduct.

The path now led through meadows by the river, which had quite changed its character, glistening mud and lines of debris showing that I had reached the tidal Wye. Tintern Parva church makes a modest appearance, seen across the fields. There has been a church here since before the Conquest, but the original was destroyed and rebuilt at around 1080. There is some typical herringbone masonry on view in the north wall of the nave. As with so many old churches, the Victorians got their hands on it and restored many of its old features into oblivion. Nevertheless, its quiet, dignified charm and simplicity make it a most attractive little building – and there are some quite startling reminders that the tidal river is liable to flood. Brass plaques on the chancel arch record flood levels.

From the church, the walk took me up to the main road lined with the hotels of Tintern. There is not much space between steep hillside and river but every inch is used, for, just up ahead, lay the famous abbey. This was not, even in its heyday, one of the great, important abbeys, in the sense that it was a centre of political power, but it was wealthy and, since the dissolution, it has acted on the imagination of thousands of visitors in a way that few other great religious houses could match. It began as a simple building in 1131, endowed by the Norman lord of Chepstow, and was handed over to the Cistercian monks, who were as rigorous in their austerity as in their purity. That was to change over the years, as wealth poured in from benefactors and the proceeds of a steadily growing estate. There is little either simple or austere about the site we see today, dominated by the great church built at the end of the thirteenth century. This is Gothic at its soaring best, and the loss of the roof has, if anything, contributed to its air of delicacy and lightness. Released from their loads, the high-pointed arches leap towards the sky, pillars stand as beautiful monoliths and the window tracery frames a

The Abbey Church at Tintern. The Abbey began as a simple affair in the twelfth century, but became steadily richer and grander, reaching a pinnacle with the construction of the magnificent church at the end of the thirteenth century.

shifting pattern of sunlight on the hillside where once it held darkening glass. Small wonder that it seemed the ideal spot to lovers of picturesque beauty. Yet Gilpin, the arch apostle of the movement, was not altogether happy. Ideally, he would have preferred less regularity, more ruin. The beauty of the west wall had little appeal, and he complained of the 'vulgarity' of its shape. Gilpin contemplated reducing that regularity with a hammer, but fortunately he changed his mind before any of its beauty was lost.

The appeal of the abbey church is obvious and immediate and was the inspiration for a famous poem by the best known of the Wye tourists, William Wordsworth. It represents, however, only the centrepiece of the monastic community, and an even wider community grew out beyond that. It is no longer easy to piece together the pattern of buildings surrounding the church, which have mostly been reduced to low walls. Size gives some idea of which were the living quarters for the various groups: monks, lay brothers, and novices. One section, where divisions into rooms can be plainly seen, represents the abbot's private chambers and the adjoining hall where he could entertain his guests. Other large areas are devoted to the infirmary and the kitchen block. A series of low tunnels shows how sophisticated the abbey was, for they carried water to the area and took sewage away. Life here was a good deal more sanitary than in most grand houses in the surrounding area.

The abbey was a great spiritual centre, and a place of considerable influence until the dissolution was ordered by Henry VIII and monastic life came to an end in 1536. But the life of Tintern itself did not end, it simply moved into a new phase. Tintern was chosen as the site where a new wireworks was to be established. Originally it was intended to work in brass, but the idea never developed, and instead the valley became one of the leading centres for the production of iron wire. We have really arrived at the start of the story, parts of which I had already collected along the way. It helps to explain the furnace in the woods, and the ponds from which water was released to power giant hammers for working metal. It even ties right back to the very start of the walk, and the fields of sheep with their young lambs. Wool was the great trade of Tudor Britain but, before it could be spun into yarn it had to be carded. The fibres were aligned by dragging the wool between wooden, hand-held boards studded with wire. It was to supply the wire for carding that the Tintern works were established.

The most important sites lie some way up the Angidy valley above Tintern, but something at least remains down by the river. The Royal George Hotel was originally home to the masters of the Lower Forge wireworks from 1720 until nearly the end of the nineteenth century. You can just make out part of the 'hammer pond' where water was stored, though a good deal of it has been built over to make a car park, and the dam which held the water back now lies under the main road. Across the road is a stone building which was probably the original forge, but was later used as a corn mill and then as a saw mill: water power is very versatile. Between the time when the monks left the abbey and the tourists came to view its ruins, this whole river valley rang with the sound of giant hammers pounding metal. The river itself was busy with trade as the barges made their way up from Chepstow, and something from those days remains in the small dock cut out of the river bank by the forge. One further, if somewhat later, survivor from the wireworks is the girder footbridge across the river, which connected the Wireworks Tramway to the Wye Valley Railway. Horses were used on this tramway right up to the 1930s. There is so much to see here apart from the obvious beauties of the abbey church, that I was kept fully occupied for the rest of the afternoon, leaving the last few miles of my walk for the following day.

Next morning I left the road to climb up the hill overlooking the river. Again, as at Whitebrook, the track is well laid out and shows every sign of once having been a packhorse route. It is a good steady climb to shake down the bacon and eggs, and the efforts of the climb were rewarded by an interesting site at the top of the hill. Here I found a jumble of squared-off stones and a number of mounds, each of which had a regular shape. No natural erosion could have produced such an effect, and everything suggests that this was once a settlement, though there was nothing left to indicate a possible date.

The walk continued along the top of Black Cliff, at the division between two landscapes. To the east the land fell away towards the river, its slopes blanketed in trees, and the woodland stretched a little way back from the edge. To the west, the forest had been cleared leaving rough pasture for the grazing sheep. The woodland itself had been coppiced, and I could see quite clearly how the tree trunks had been cut right back, practically to ground level, to allow new shoots to grow. But timber was not the only resource of these woods. From time to time there were signs of digging and quarrying, and the woodland names give precise indications of what was going on, for Limekiln Wood was followed by Minepit Wood, and there was no problem about deciding which was which. All I had to do was look at the rock beneath my feet. At one point I could see a reddish-brown stone, not unlike a very dark sandstone: this is ironstone, the raw material for the Tintern furnaces. Elsewhere I saw the grey limestone and found a ruined lime kiln in the woods. The need for packhorse routes now seemed obvious.

The woods had another significance, for they became part of a regular picturesque tourist itinerary. The early tourists appreciated a guiding hand to lead them towards the best viewpoints – much as I appreciated having a waymarked route to follow. A local landowner, Valentine Morris, laid out the Piercefield Walks at the end of the eighteenth century and steps were later cut to take visitors to the top of Wynd Cliff, a limestone buttress rising 213 metres (700 feet) above the river. Special viewing points were constructed, tiny grottoes were added to embellish nature, and, at one point, the path actually tunnels through the rock. It is all just as attractive today as it was two centuries ago, offering some of the finest river views in the whole of Britain. But the most exciting view came near the end of the walk when, through a clearing, I caught my first view of Chepstow with its castle battlements rising high above the town. Soon the woods began to thin and the steady accumulation of cans and wrapping paper announced the arrival of civilization.

It was now a short walk down through the grounds of a school and past one curious anachronism. A rather grand house boasts a fine set of wrought-iron gates and an avenue of trees, but modern road building has cut off the avenue leaving the gates as useless ornaments. Beyond that the path turned down to follow the line of the moat of Chepstow Castle. Superficially this is not unlike Goodrich Castle writ large. But it was soon apparent that Chepstow is far more complex, and even as I

Gothic at its towering best: the pointed arches line the nave of the Abbey Church at Tintern.

walked round the walls, evidence of different building styles and periods appeared. There was the gaunt square block of the Great Tower at the upper end of the castle and rounded towers, similar to those at Goodrich at the lower end. The best way to approach the castle is to go inside and head straight through the lower bailey to the next line of walls. These mark the original limit of William fitz Osbern's castle, begun in 1067 immediately after the Conquest. Clearly, the strategic importance of this promontory guarding the entrance to the Wye Valley had been quickly recognized. The wall itself was altered by William Marshall around 1200, with the addition of round towers and the present arched entrance. Once inside, it is easy to see the defensive plan. The Wye cliffs are all that was needed on the river side, and the roughly triangular site kept building work to a minimum. The Great Tower dominates everything. Its style is unmistakeably Norman and it speaks more clearly of defence than of domestic comfort. This, with the upper ward behind it, represents the total building plan of the first castle. In time, defence was improved, but comfort was improved as well. A barbican was added to the upper ward, and a new tower was also completed with rooms for guests. The most significant change, however, came with the addition of the lower bailey in the thirteenth century with a noteable improvement in creature comforts for the castle occupants. There were new domestic quarters, and most importantly, a very grand new hall, in which some of the original painted decoration has survived. The fortress was still a fortress, but growing prosperity made it a comfortable one.

This was the end of the walk, but from the castle I could look out over the town of Chepstow and see just how it was set into a loop of the river and how its plan and its defences were tied to the castle. The main road stretches up from the river to the town walls and the town gate which was rebuilt in the sixteenth century. I began at Goodrich by asking why the castle was there, but here the answer was even plainer. To the south, the Wye meets the Severn, the great King's Highway of Severn as it was once known, while the Wye itself forms the natural boundary between England and Wales. It would have been amazing if a castle had not been built here, and equally astounding if a town had not grown up beneath its protective walls. And that at first glance might have seemed to be that, had I not walked the Valley and seen the Wye as a trade route serving important industrial communities. It was this that brought Chepstow its prosperity and, when I looked down to the river, I could still people it in imagination with wharves and warehouses, ships and barges. Ultimately, it all came back to the river: as trade route, as frontier, and, not least importantly, as a thing of beauty.

The two churches of Swaffham Prior: St Mary's on the left and St Cyriac and Julietta on the right.

One of the many elaborate, timber-framed buildings of Lavenham.

WATER AND WOOL
Wicken Fen to Lavenham, 38 miles (61 km), OS maps 154,155.

This walk proved, if nothing else, that even the most carefully laid plans and the most meticulous preparations do not always lead to the desired results. My original route made considerable use of footpaths across fields but I had not made allowances for the enthusiastic ploughing policies of the local farmers. Time and again, a path was invisible beneath deep clay furrows or standing crops and, by the end, I was rerouting the whole walk on to minor roads which, happily, often turned out to have wide grass verges for comfortable walking. It was all a great contrast to the last, waymarked route along the Wye Valley. It was a contrast, too, in another way for East Anglia does not produce much in the way of hard slogs up steep hillsides. Not that it is all flat – very far from it – and, indeed, this was a walk which once again showed with great clarity how the nature of the land has determined the ways in which people can use it.

I began at the National Trust Nature Reserve at Wicken Fen on one of those days which show East Anglia at its best. Huge clouds pushed before the wind sailed from horizon to horizon like a heavenly fleet review, to appear in repeat performance at my feet, reflected in the brown, peaty water that can be found all over this region. But it was water, not clouds, that formed the true key to this landscape. One thing was clear from the very first, the countryside which I could see stretching away in all directions had been formed by human control of the wetland. Ruler-straight ditches and channels squared off the land into separate areas, and the one where I was to start represents only one phase in the development of the fens. This area of Wicken Fen is principally visited by birdwatchers and it is easy to understand why for, even when you cannot see the birds, the whole fen echoes with the mixed chorus ranging from the deep trumpetings of the geese to the high melody of the skylark. But I was there because Wicken is the last remnant of one particular type of fen. It is not strictly wild and, to understand just what you are looking at, you have to know what the true wild fen was and how man has set about changing it.

Thousands of years ago, this whole area was covered in dense forest. Then around 5000 years ago, the climate grew noticeably wetter: the sea began to encroach further on to the land, rivers swelled, and lakes formed. The great trees fell and vegetation rotted to form peat through which the brown waters oozed. The woodland which had once covered some 2500 square miles (6500 sq km) became a swamp, out of which rose a few habitable islands such as that on which Ely now stands. Over the centuries, various sections of this fenland were drained to be used for agriculture, but even the undrained fen was put to use. It was a valuable source of all kinds of useful commodities. Reed and sedge

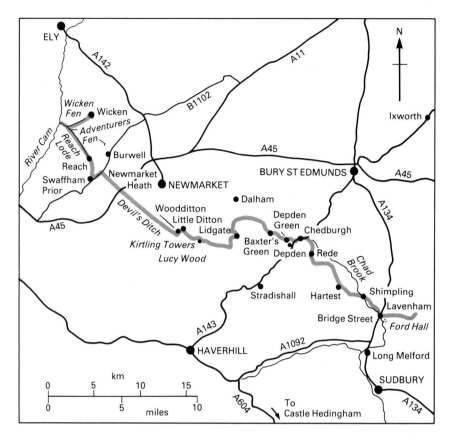

could be harvested for thatching; wildfowl could be caught for food; fish – and especially eels – were to be found in the water. Then there was the peat itself which could be cut and dried for fuel. But the more peat you cut, the more the water will collect, and locals had to balance these different factors to make the best use of the fenland. In time, as we shall see, fen drainage spread virtually throughout the area, to everywhere, in fact, except the area of Wicken. This is the last remnant of the old managed fenland and, left to its own devices, it would very rapidly take on a quite different appearance.

The most obvious features of the area are the broad trackways, or droves, which run across the wet areas. These provide reasonably dry access for peat cutters and reed harvesters – though in wet weather, a walk down a drove can seem like a walk through black treacle as you sink up to your ankles with every step. Some of these droves date back at least as far as the sixteenth century when the fen was divided between many different owners, much as the familiar common fields were at the same period. The area was not entirely left to be managed in the old way, for the steady removal of peat led inexorably to flooding and the spread of marsh plants. In the 1840s, there were attempts to drain this last area of fen but, because of the drainage pattern in the surrounding areas, the would-be improvers found they were too late on the scene. The natural drainage line was blocked. And if water cannot be run away downhill, then some means has to be found of lifting it uphill. This was true of the whole area, and the eighteenth-century answer, borrowed from across the Channel in Holland, was the windmill. And this was the first prominent mark to which I headed.

The tiny mill is typical of hundreds once scattered through the region. This is a smock mill, that is, a mill with a wooden base, topped

Wicken Fen wind pump. This simple windmill was used to drive a scoop wheel, set inside the semicircular wooden cover behind the main building. The wheel, as its name suggests, scooped up water for drainage.

by a rotating cap which carries the sails. The sails are turned to the wind by means of the tail pole hanging down from the cap. The machinery could scarcely be simpler. Gears convert the drive from the sails to turn a scoop wheel. As the name suggests, the wheel turns and scoops up water from a lower level and deposits it into a new channel at a higher level. The Wicken Fen mill has been moved to this site, but it is still possible to see how the system works.

Walking round the fen, I found a tremendous variety of habitats, which are home to a rich collection of plant and animal life, and which explain why Wicken Fen is as it is today. At the end of the last century, the undrained fen attracted the interest of naturalists and it was taken over by the National Trust to become the country's first nature reserve. The Trust have also preserved the features of the old managed landscape, showing many different stages of development of the land and the uses to which it was put. Square pits mark where in the last century clay was dug out from under the peat for brick-making. You can see the greyish-white slimy clay and, in the surrounding area, you can see the greyish-white bricks that were made from it. Scrubland, dotted with oak and ash, shows how the woodland which once dominated the region could easily take over again given the right conditions. This is a partially dried area, known as a 'carr'. Elsewhere, where water levels are higher, sedge, reed, and marsh hay thrive. There are even reminders of a more ancient landscape in the bog oaks, massive trunks that remained waterlogged for thousands of years until unearthed during attempts to clear the land.

A circuit of the reserve eventually brought me to the south side and the Wicken Lode. The Lode represents the first type of system introduced to control the water in the fens. It is an artificial channel dug to carry the water away into the River Cam. It also became a trade route, a navigable waterway along which lighters could travel bringing supplies to the villages and taking away the important crops of reed, sedge, and peat. At the Lode I could see the differences in levels: the Wicken side of undrained land was notably higher than that across the water. This is Adventurers Fen, a name which itself has something to say about the history of the area.

The first lodes were constructed as far back as Roman times, but conditions deteriorated through the Dark Ages. In spite of sporadic attempts during Tudor times to reclaim the wetlands again, nothing much happened until the 1630s when the major landowners banded together to work on a comprehensive drainage scheme for the whole region. They risked a considerable amount of capital and gained themselves the name 'adventurers'. Their work was not universally

applauded. The fen men saw 'improvement' as the loss of ancient rights to fish and fowl, to peat and reed: it was a fenland equivalent to the enclosure movement that was simultaneously beginning to affect the old common land elsewhere in the country. The adventurers straightened rivers to speed the flow of water and dug new drainage channels. As they dug and improved, so the locals, known as 'fen tigers' attacked and destroyed their work where and when they could. As with enclosure riots the end was inevitable, for the forces of the adventurers were stronger than those of the fen men. In later centuries the windmills were brought in to supplement the drainage work. Adventurers Fen, like Wicken Fen, stood apart from the general movement, remaining undrained right up to World War 2 when the government declared it was needed for agriculture. It was then drained and one can see the effect in the land level differences. After the war, it reverted to the National Trust and, what I was now looking at, was drained land gradually reverting to water and reedbeds.

I left the reserve and walked up the bank of the lode, and then crossed it by a neat wooden footbridge to follow Burwell Lode to Upware, where more of the story of the changing fens began to emerge. Various intriguing shapes could be seen at the end of the waterway. Firstly, straddling the lode itself, was what in silhouette looked like a giant notice board, and alongside it a building with two levels. The first object soon revealed itself to be a lock. That the lode was navigable was obvious from the lines of moored boats, and here it joins the River Cam. The lock is controlled by conventional mitred lock gates at the river end, but at the lode end is a guillotine gate, where the gate itself rises and falls

The attractive village of Reach, which has settled back to a peaceful life after centuries of being a busy inland port.

vertically. It emphasizes the dual importance of the lode for drainage and transport. But the odd building alongside is very much concerned with drainage. The windmill was fine in its way, but it only worked when the wind blew and its power was limited. The nineteenth-century solution was the steam engine. On closer inspection, the building was seen to have three parts: a low boiler house, a tall engine house, and another low section which held a scoop wheel. The boiler house is just what the name suggests, the engine house once held a massive beam engine and that drove the wheel, big brother to the one seen at Wicken Fen. The machinery has, alas, all gone but a survivor of this type of system can still be seen at Stretham about 3 miles (5 km) away. A new modern pumping house can be seen across the lode, for this is a continuous story and, without the pumps, the fenland would sink again beneath the waters.

I walked on, back down the opposite bank and then followed Reach Lode to the village of Reach. It is now established or, perhaps one should say, almost established that this was one of the Roman lodes. The evidence consists of an abundance of Roman finds on either side of the waterway, and it is certainly true that this was an established lode in the Middle Ages when few, if any, new schemes were being put in hand. There is little, however, to distinguish this from any of the other navigable drains in the area. What is very clear is that it passes through well-drained agricultural land: it has been a success. All around was rich, black soil, a chocolate-coloured landscape of wide fields, dotted by farms that have achieved a measure of prosperity from the reclaimed land. What was also clear as I walked along the side of the lode was that the land was rising up before me – not a great hill but a very perceptible rise, and quite sufficient to lift the land above the water level. The fens were coming to an end.

At Reach itself, the waterway divided to pass on either side of a promontory, and this is quite significant, for it suggests the need for a good deal of water space to hold a large number of craft. It may not look like a very important feature today but, looked at on the map, there is a pattern to be seen: a navigable lode of considerable antiquity, leading to a navigable river, and ultimately to the sea. This dead end on the edge of the fens could once have been an inland port of some importance. The thought was confirmed as I walked up the lane from the water's edge to find the name 'The Hythe', the old English word for harbour. It requires something of an act of imagination to see this as the East Anglian Liverpool of the Middle Ages, but that is what it was, and boats traded here well into the twentieth century. Ruins of old buildings can be seen on the promontory, and there are signs of former importance in the grander village buildings. One particularly fine building on The Hythe shows its medieval origins as clearly as it shows its rather four-square, unconvincing addition of a Victorian wing.

In spite of its few grand buildings, the village itself shows scant signs of its former importance, and some of the visual evidence is a little misleading. The church, for example, is almost insignificant, a low, drab structure that clearly proclaims its nineteenth-century origins. There are hints of better things. The large village green was once home to an important fair. Some of the village houses have quite elaborate pargetting, decorative plasterwork, and there is a hint that once Reach looked on itself as quite an urban settlement, for there is some very townish engraved glass in the pub door. Yet it has declined from the days when almost every other house was an inn, and trade flowed. There is at least a reminder of what that trade was in the latter years, for the fields to the south-west of the village show unmistakeable signs of quarrying. This was where they once extracted the chalky-clay known as 'clunch', widely used for buildings in the region. But there is one other feature of note at the head of the village green – a giant mound of earth with a deep ditch alongside which heads off towards the south-east. It is one of the most remarkable features of this landscape, and I should be seeing it in all its glory later. But, for the moment, my path lay up the minor road to Swaffham Prior.

The climb up from Reach is gentle, but the extra height opens out huge vistas, in which the most obvious feature was Ely cathedral set up on its mound that rises above the flat lands of the fens. But another feature, closer at hand, aroused my curiosity. Over to the east I could see a great V cut into the land and, if I had been asked to identify it at first sight, I would have no hesitation in saying 'railway cutting' and that first notion seemed to be confirmed for the road did pass over a disused line. But, for the time being, my attention was concentrated on the Swaffham Prior skyline straight ahead. The remains of a windmill were easily distinguished and so was a massive water tower, but two other towers, very close together were more of a puzzle. That little problem was left on one side for a moment as the road entered the outskirts of the village which showed characteristics that would remain as recognizable features for virtually the whole of the walk. Building materials used for the older houses were all those available locally and that meant timber-framing and in an area virtually devoid of stone, brick, and flint. But, when I reached the churchyard, the mystery of the two towers was explained, for it contained not one church but two. The question still to be answered was why there should be two churches and the answer is tied to the story of the village itself.

In Norman times the village was divided between three sets of owners: the Prior of Ely, Hardwin de Scalers, and a group of three anonymous knights from Brittany. Ely had the earliest claim and endowed a Saxon church, St Mary's, of which nothing now is visible. The present St Mary's has a simple twelfth-century core, which was later enlarged by the addition of aisles and a very grand, three-storey tower. The latter begins as a simple square, with an octagon added above that and topped by a polygonal tower of somewhat later date. The Norman landowners of the rest of the village, either through an excess of piety or pride, decided that their section needed a church of its own. St Cyriac and Julietta was founded around 1250. The story of the two churches now becomes decidedly complex. The parishes were united in the seventeenth century, and it was decided that one church was quite sufficient. The nave of St Cyriac's was demolished and the bell tower was left in solitary grandeur. Then, 100 years later, St Mary's was struck by lightning and, instead of restoring that, a new nave was built for St Cyriac's. The distinctly odd result was a medieval tower stuck on the end of a plain Georgian church. Fortunes wavered again. It was St Cyriac's turn to deteriorate and then to be ignored, and restoration work was done on St Mary's. And that is how matters stand today. St Mary's has all the airs of a fine old church, boasting numerous excellent monumental brasses and some strange modern stained-glass windows. These windows deserve more than a passing glance. In the north aisle, they celebrate the end of World War 1, not with images of peace but in a burst of patriotic fervour. Cannon roar and aeroplanes bomb, raining destruction on the Beastly Hun. And is there a church anywhere else in Europe that depicts ladies filling shells in a munitions factory? Neighbouring St Cyriac's is left as a handsome, but echoingly empty box.

Swaffham Prior encourages lingering, and linger I did through an early evening when the sky turned to a cloudless blue and the bright spring sunshine seemed to offer splendid omens for the next day's walking. It proved, alas, a delusion. Morning brought an oppressive, leaden sky and torrential rain driven on by an east wind. I restarted my journey at the churchyard by crossing the stile to follow the back lane above the old tenement plots. This old village pattern was a common one, with house plots stretching back from the main street to a lane beyond the old boundary walls. Then I turned through a modern housing development expecting to take a clearly marked footpath off to the east. It was the first of my disappointments – for in place of the footpath was a field of rich dark mud. So I turned northward on the road that led towards Burwell, which at least produced some compensation. Swaffham Prior can boast two windmills to set beside its two churches. One was a smock mill, more or less in ruins, but the other, a tower mill was in fine condition. The other pleasing feature on the road was a rather smart, classically designed pumping station of 1939 with its attendant water tower.

It was a mercifully short walk down the rather busy B1102 before I reached the great V in the land that I had seen from the Reach road – not a railway cutting, but the Devil's Ditch. Seen close up, it is quite remarkable, a deep, steep-sided ditch with a high bank along the eastern side. It was clearly defensive and would have made a formidable obstacle. It was easy to see how it was constructed with the spoil from the ditch being piled up to form the bank. It was also easy to see how it worked as a barrier at this end at least, for it ran straight down to Reach

The massive bank and V-shaped ditch of the Devil's Ditch near Swaffham Prior. This defensive barrier stretches from the edge of the fens to what was the impenetrable forest beyond Newmarket Heath.

The high earthworks and deep ditch of the Devil's Ditch stretching across Newmarket Heath. To the left of the picture is the July Course and the National Stud.

and the edge of the natural obstacle of the fens. What is not so easily determined is when it was built. The one thing we can say with any certainty is that it is post-Roman for, when sections were removed for modern road building, Roman artefacts were found under the bank. It must, then, date from the Dark Ages period when England was divided between warring factions. It would seem logical to assume that the impetus for such a major work must have come from a period of great upheaval in the history of the country. Two possible events suggest themselves. The first is the great battle of Mons Badonicus of *c.* 500, a somewhat shadowy event for no-one knows where Mons Badonicus was nor are the protagonists clearly identified. What is known is that the Saxon mercenaries of south-east England rebelled and, after the battle, they were driven back towards East Anglia. The successful British forces were, it is thought, led by Arthur, a chieftain whose fame has come down to us in a much changed form as King Arthur of the Round Table. Turning again from legend to fact, we may have the defeated Saxons setting up a barrier to defend their new homeland of East Anglia. In the seventh century, the Anglo-Saxon kingdoms of Anglia were well established but were under threat from the powerful King Penda of Mercia. The threat was real enough, so the construction of defences must also have seemed of great importance in the middle of the seventh century. In the event, they were to prove insufficient to hold back the Mercians. Anglia fell at the end of the century.

On a clear day, the walk along the top of the Ditch offers splendid views, a high-level route across low-lying country. It was less appealing when walking into the eye of an east wind throwing rain into your face. Uncharitably perhaps, I wondered why anyone should wish to attack this wet soggy land or bother to defend it. But I could at least see that I was passing through quite rich farming country with clay overlying the chalk that formed a slimy grey thread along the top of the Ditch. Beyond the busy main A45 road lay the great flat expanse of Newmarket Heath. If you scramble down from the bank and walk out on to the heath proper, you find a wonderfully soft, springy turf under foot, and that has been its main attraction for nearly 400 years. On any day of the year, the principal industry of the area is on display, for even on a vile, wet day in April, the strings of racehorses were out, steaming from their gallops across the heath. To the east I could see the grandstands of the Rowley Mile Course; to the west the July Course and the National Stud. The first horse races were held here in 1619 in the reign of James I. I was walking a Dark Ages defence and striding across the prosperous landscape of a newly united kingdom.

At the next main road, there was a glimpse of racing's other aspect, with a set of jumps. The Ditch, meanwhile, carried on marching across the landscape until it met another embankment at much the same level. The newcomer carried the old Great Eastern Railway, which is still the main Cambridge to Newmarket line. Railway history books often refer to the immense labour of the railway navvies who built these great embankments using quite primitive equipment. This particular line shows, in fact, a very good example of 'cut and fill', cuttings being driven through the rising ground, and the spoil being used to build up the banks across the valleys. But, if the work of the railway navvies is impressive, how much more impressive is the work of the anonymous builders of the Devil's Ditch, working with even more primitive equipment. An immense work force must have been needed and a good deal of organizational skill. It says a good deal about the power of the kingdom of the Angles.

Beyond the cutting, the Ditch became a raised path through a narrow spinney, which I was about to welcome as cover against the rain, when the rain eased off. Perversely, this only added to my sense of annoyance at the vagaries of the climate. The nature of the countryside was now changing once again, as the flat heathland was left behind, and the land began to heave and roll in steady undulations. Isolated woods now dotted the landscape in an apparently random manner, and farmland was marked off by hedgerows. When the Ditch crossed the next minor road, it formed the boundary of Sketchworth Park, and marked a definite division in the nature of the land. On one side was the manor house and park, now home to a stud farm – all immaculate fields, neat fences, and stable blocks built to a standard that would be no disgrace to an estate for humans. On the other side was farmland and a large block of dark green, a modern conifer plantation. It was the bit between, however, that was most significant in terms of the history of the region.

The Ditch path is a narrow way through dense woodland, dotted with massive trees, notably beech. Ridge and ditch have made this narrow strip impossible for cultivation, so natural forces have taken over to show how this whole area would have looked if left to its own devices – and how it looked in the past. The Devil's Ditch now makes a complete sense, for it could be seen as joining the marshes and swamps of the undrained fens to an area of dense, almost impenetrable forest. All that now remains of the ancient forest is the strip along the Ditch, and the patches that dot the surrounding fields. The function of the woods was equally clear, for rabbits scampered across the path in front of me, while pheasants strutted along the edges of the fields. The copses give the game their homes, and the dull crack of a distant shotgun showed that this was not merely an act of landowner's benevolence.

From the end of the Ditch, a path led across the fields to a prominent water tower of Woodditton. The village itself seems at first glance to offer little of interest, yet that paradoxically is just where its main interest lies. Where is the centre? Where is the focal point of growth? The church is isolated to the north and one is left with a straggle of houses down an insignificant main street. This is by no means unique in the area, and what we seem to have is an undefined village surrounded by a scatter of farms, based on individual efforts to carve out a portion of the forest. My route went on to Little Ditton and then turned south on to the bridleway that headed across the fields to one of the few really grand buildings hereabouts, Kirtling Towers. Even so, it is now no more than a reminder of the greater splendours of the past. First, there was a castle here, of which only the moat remains. After that, there was a grand mansion which was pulled down in the nineteenth century, leaving only the gatehouse standing. Tall turrets of red brick provide the name of Kirtling Towers, and their rich detailing shows that they were intended to impress rather than provide defence. The building dates from 1530 and demonstrates as clearly as can be the faith that landowners had in the Tudor peace.

The road now wended its way past the edge of Lucy Wood to a crossroads and the Queen's Head pub, which proved to be a good deal more than a pleasant place to stop and enjoy very traditional home-cooked food and an equally traditional pint, for it also provided a footnote to the history of Kirtling. The importance of the grand house is confirmed by the fact that Queen Elizabeth I came to stay here in 1588, and such was the size of her retinue that a new house had to be constructed to take the overflow from the mansion. That building became the Queen's Head and, if its age was not immediately apparent from the outside, it became more obvious once I went inside, where a

The ornate red-brick turrets of Kirtling Towers rise above the trees. Grand though the building seems, this was no more than a gatehouse to the even more splendid mansion, now sadly destroyed.

log fire roared in the vast hearth. It has nothing to do with history, but I did like the 'log basket', a fine brass kettle drum, minus its skin.

Fortified by food and ale and dried off by the fire, I went on in more cheerful mood heading off to the east and the Suffolk boundary. A pattern was soon set for the rest of that day and the next, of a gentle stroll along quiet lanes through undulating countryside. Some of the distinctive features are obvious from the map: narrow twisting roads, a spattering of isolated farms and small hamlets with, between, small patches of woodland. It is, or was, a very English landscape, but recent years have brought considerable change to the face of the country. Old boundaries have disappeared, hedgerows have been rooted up and, if the overall effect is not quite that of the prairie farmland found in much of East Anglia, it is quite close to it. Yet the old has not quite been expunged: signs of hedge and ditch remain, which show the patterns established in an earlier period of widespread change when the square fields of enclosure were formed. There are indications too of older field patterns, but these are difficult to see for the enclosure movement began a long time ago in these parts and was already well advanced by the end of the Tudor period. Water plays almost as important a role as it does in the fens. The heavy clay would be unmanageable without adequate drainage, so ditches were dug, that acted as both boundaries and drains. The clay removed in the process was then piled up to form protective banks that guarded the crops against the winds which, I was all too aware, whistle across this land. And round this system of bank and ditch the roads still wind their tortuous way.

The villages may be small, but it soon became apparent that each had its own unique character, and that differences from one to the next can often be traced back to features which are still apparent today. For the rest of the description of the walk, I shall be concentrating mainly on the differences to be found from place to place and pointing out those sections where the most significant landscape features are most clearly seen. So if a stretch seems to go by with no significant points being made, this does not mean that I found it dull, simply that a particular point is better explained elsewhere.

The one thing you rarely find in this part of the world is a truly modern feature. Vicarage Farm is certainly an old farmstead site, but there is nothing in the least bit old about what stands there today. What you have, in fact, is an excellent example of a modern farm which sits most comfortably in the landscape, yet has made no attempt to ape older styles. Too often the twentieth-century contribution to the agricultural landscape consists of four-square metal boxes for barns and suburban villas set down among fields as farmhouses. Here was a real sense of style, a building which, in its bold use of planes and angles to create an intriguing facade, declares itself to be very much of the late twentieth century but which, by using local materials such as timber, can be seen as part of a continuing tradition.

A mile further on, a turning brought me to the village of Lidgate, which soon turned out to be a most intriguing spot. Here instead of the somewhat incoherent pattern I had seen so far, a focal point immediately presented itself to view, the church sat on the crest of the hill. The village itself huddles for shelter at the foot of the hill, houses grouped round the large village pond and then spreading out along the road to Stradishall. Village houses proclaim their age in timber frames, and many of them are jettied. These are houses where the upper storey projects above the lower floor. It was once common in towns where space was at a premium, and in some medieval streets, such as the Shambles in York, you will find upper storeys that seem almost to touch the houses across the way. In the country, however, it was rather more of a mark of opulence, suggesting that the owner was a cut above his bucolic neighbours. So tiny Lidgate shows signs of prosperity as well as age. A clue to that prosperity can be found by the church. It is not just the natural hill that gives it its prominence, for when I got closer I could see that the hilltop itself had actually been raised by means of an artificial mound. And not only that, when I walked round the churchyard, I found it to be enclosed within a moat. Where the church now stands was

Lidgate church rises high above the village, its height increased by the fact that it stands on the motte of a Norman castle. The water in the foreground marks the remains of the moat.

once a motte and bailey, or mound and enclosure, the oldest and simplest form of Norman castle. Lidgate was once a centre of local power – and it seems to have been an important spot for quite some while for aerial photographs show that a large Roman villa once stood here.

From the church, a lane led down to the Dalham road, which I followed up to Copley Grove before turning east again for Ousden. Here the pattern was very different with the church virtually isolated at one end of the village. Elsewhere this would lead to all kinds of speculation about shrunken villages and changing patterns of development, but this seems such a common feature in Suffolk that it scarcely excites attention. The church itself, however, is quite interesting, like a complete lesson in architectural history, for it started in the eleventh century, and bits kept being added. Apart from that, the main feature in the village was a fine row of flint cottages. I left the village to head off for Baxter's Green and Depden, through countryside which consisted of isolated farms joined by a complex web of roads and lanes. Sometimes, as at Baxter's Green, a road heads off to nothing but an apparent dead end, but is then continued as a footpath. Each farm has its direct link to its neighbour, and only the most important of these linking tracks have survived as modern roads. I followed a road which declared its age by its tall, impressive bordering hedge.

Depden, however, posed some very interesting problems. I began by walking up the road past the council houses to an area shown on the map as having a moat and a hall. The hall was there alright, a very typical timber-framed hall-house, but the moat was on a private estate. What I did not see, but expected to, was any sign of a path through to the church. I retraced my steps to Depden Green, a big triangular green surrounded by a scatter of old houses, and then walked on round to Depden itself, which seemed a much later development. It was here, however, that I finally found the official path to the church, a narrow, muddy footpath past a farm and through a small wood. I also found a sturdy wooden post carrying an equally sturdy sign bearing the word 'footpath' and pointing straight at the unbroken furrows of a large field. Frustration was compounded when I found the church to be locked, and no indication of how a key might be obtained. So I was left puzzling over this strange arrangement: an isolated group of large houses, one of them moated; a village based on a green, but sparsely populated, and a separate hamlet which now has the only access to the church. It is tempting to think of church and hall as centrepieces of an ancient village that decayed, perhaps during the Black Death, to be followed by a new settlement round the green, which in turn was superseded by later builders who preferred to be near the main road. I have no evidence to support the theory, and only detailed local research could produce the facts – and might not even then. For the time being at least, I was free to speculate and, having abandoned all hope of finding a usable footpath, I settled reluctantly for a short walk along the main road to Chedburgh and the end of the day's excursion.

The next day began mercifully dry, and the sun even managed a few half-hearted appearances as I continued down the main road, which now forms the obvious axis for new development, whether for factory or nursery garden. I was not unhappy to turn off on the road to Rede. Again the road wound and wriggled, often turning through right-angles – a route dictated by patterns of land ownership rather than the convenience of travellers. Near Lodge Farm, for example, an almost direct route exists as a footpath, but the road bends to meet the farm and then turns back again to pick up the direct route to Rede. This is another hamlet grouped round a church and green. Immediately beyond is Pykards Hall, timber framed and coloured a lovely rich red. This is the

A tug-of-war on the green at Hartest on the day of the village fete. This picture-postcard village still has a real life and vitality.

colour known as 'Suffolk pink', and is not a paint but a lime wash that, with repeated applications, weathers to a condition where the walls seem to be dyed, so deeply does the colour penetrate into the fabric.

This is a wonderfully open section of the walk with wide views over the countryside, but things are not always quite what they seem. A large house by a crossroads looked from a distance as if it would be just another plain, sturdy farmhouse but, when I reached Scole Gate, I found it to be a very old house with mullioned windows. Beyond that, the road wiggled on its way again through fields marked by bank and ditch to the village of Hartest sitting comfortably and snugly in a deep hollow. This is everyone's idea of just what an English village should be. A large green is surrounded by a rich mixture of houses, many decked out in colour wash. The village butcher was still trading, not yet having succumbed to the supermarket of the nearest town, and an old inn and the church stood at the apex of the triangular green. If there is something of a self-satisfied air to Hartest, then it does have a lot to be smug about. There is scarcely a false note here, even though the buildings cover a wide range of styles and types, from small, jettied half-timbered houses to later Gothic. Details prove as pleasing as the overall effect. Near the inn, for example, is a close-studded, timber-framed building, that is, one in which the vertical timbers are set close together. This is not unusual, but what makes it special is the use of bricks in a herring-bone pattern as an infill. But perhaps the most pleasing feature of Hartest is that it is more than a mere show place, it is a community. Goal posts show that the village green is really used and, when I went into the church, I found an army of villagers scrubbing and polishing in the annual spring clean.

Climbing up the steep hill out of Hartest, I was rewarded with fine views and the clearest indications yet of the character of this landscape. Dotted all over the countryside are patches of woodland, whose timber once provided the main building material of the area. But there are hints of other materials, too, in names such as Brickhouse Farm and Kiln Farm. Grander halls sit among the smaller farms and everywhere there are signs of the old divisions in the land. The roadway, which had seldom been straight at any point in the walk, became ever more convoluted, and was marked by deeper ditches, higher banks and, in places, dense hedgerows. There is little suggestion here of the neat parcelling out of the land of the eighteenth-century enclosure movement, but rather of a pattern first set much further back in history. Records show that I was, in fact, looking at a landscape that was much as it would have appeared in the reign of the first Elizabeth. Crops were more important than cattle and the village greens such as those of Depden and Hartest provided adequate grazing. So, outside the village there was not much need for open grazing land, and farmers set about creating the ditches that both drained and marked the fields. And from up here on the relatively high land, I could look out over those other great features of the landscape, the church towers that rise up to mark each village and hamlet. One lay in my path, the church at Shimpling, a modest place yet huge in terms of the hamlet that it serves. Between here and Bridge Street, the road was at its most twisted and the field banks at their highest.

Bridge Street earns its name, for it has been a crossing place on the Chad Brook for many centuries. The Roman road between present-day Ixworth and Long Melford came this way roughly, though not precisely, following the line of the A134. Ford Hall standing just to the south of the main road is a lovely example of a moated hall. We tend to associate moats with defence, but this is seldom the case in Suffolk. What you see is a platform of raised land on which the house is built, and around which is a water-filled ditch. The ditch had several uses – it acted as a drain, it was a useful protection against floods, it could be stocked with fish and lastly, but not necessarily least in importance, it lent an air of distinction to a property. It gave the hall something of the same status as a castle.

For the final stage of the walk, I climbed up the hill from Bridge Street and headed off to Lavenham, and it was not long before the town announced its presence. Quite suddenly, as I came to the crest of one hill, the tower of Lavenham church appeared floodlit in a shaft of brilliant sunlight. It shone like a beacon for a moment, then the clouds drifted over and the tower returned to a dull greyness, still impressing by its size but not quite the thing of glory it had been a moment before. I was glad of that brief burst of light for it showed Lavenham as it was intended to be seen, as the opulent centrepiece of a rich countryside. It encouraged me to march just a little faster over those last two or three miles. I was briefly tempted by an alternative route, along the now disused railway that provides a direct line through to the north end of Lavenham, but that would have delayed me from visiting the splendours of the church. The church won, and it was right that it should do so for it is in the church that Lavenham proclaims its message with its clearest voice.

The splendour of Lavenham church, which proclaims the wealth of a community that prospered on the wool trade of Tudor England.

I once read a piece on Lavenham which described this building as seeming like a fine city church, but that is misleading, for it gives the wrong sense of scale. Few city churches dominate their surroundings as this does. It might more aptly be termed a village cathedral, for this is a church which combines monumental size with immense richness of detail. It is a splendid example of the Perpendicular style, with its fine tower rising to a height of almost 43 metres (141 feet), while the body of the church seems to contain more glass than stone. Everything, however, speaks of wealth. Stone is not available locally so it had to be brought from further north, and once here superb craftsmen were set to work on the delicate tracery. The richest carving is to be found on the porch, predictably, for it was the gift of the church's most important patron, John de Vere, Earl of Oxford, and his emblems – the star and

Lavenham's Wool Hall was originally built for a trade guild, but was converted to become the most important merchant's trading centre in the seventeenth century.

the boar – can be seen among the carvings. The church was not built entirely or even principally out of piety, but to celebrate political events and commercial success. The de Veres proposed rebuilding the old church as a gesture to welcome the succession of the Tudors, who came to the throne after the defeat of Richard III at Bosworth Field. The church was intended as a monument to that victory, but it was the wealthiest of the local families who largely paid for its construction. They saw it as a celebration of their vast commercial success in Lavenham's greatest industry, the manufacture of woollen cloth. So the magnificence of the church stands as an emblem of Tudor political success and the clothiers' commercial enterprise. The de Veres make the first impression on visitors, but it is Thomas Spryng the Third, known as the 'great clothier', who leaves the abiding impression of having brought great beauty to this fine building. A rich wooden screen surrounds the Spryng parclose where the family are buried. But grandest of all the family bequests is the Lady Chapel. Nothing says more about the wealth of the Spryngs and, by extension, the wealth of Tudor Lavenham than the interior of this magnificent church.

Nothing really prepares you for Lavenham. A few sheep seen along the way might give rise to passing thoughts of the wool trade, but would hardly suggest this great prosperity. There are no obvious traces of the wool industry, such as you might expect to find in Yorkshire or the West of England. But here we are looking at an East Anglian industry that reached its zenith in the sixteenth century, and after that diminished and declined until only the memories remain, epitomized in the Church of Sts Peter and Paul. And it is precisely because of this sudden decline in Lavenham's fortunes that the town quite simply stopped growing. It was stopped, frozen in its period of greatest success. So what I was seeing was a basically late medieval town which, incredible as it might seem, was once one of the wealthiest in the kingdom. It ranked fourteenth in the assessment for the great tax of 1523-26, standing one place above the city of York. This was the time when the Spryng family were at the height of their powers. The decline of that family also saw the decline of the cloth trade. Its final demise came with the industrial revolution of the eighteenth century. The old industry had depended on spinners working at home, providing the yarn for skilled craftsmen – dyers, weavers, croppers – who also either worked at home or in small workshops attached to a clothier's house. The new factory industry depended on water power, which was available in plenty from the hill streams of the Pennines but not in the flat lands of East Anglia. The industry moved away, leaving the buildings as reminders of the prosperous past.

The most obvious fact that strikes every visitor to Lavenham is the great wealth of timber-framed buildings. Remembering that this was a cloth-making town, you might expect to find among them some signs of the trade, such as weavers' cottages. Such signs are not as obvious as they are in the north of England, and the best you can say is that any obviously old cottage with particularly large windows was probably used by weavers, for they needed a good light for the work on the loom. Some likely candidates turned up in Water Street. I noticed a doorway at first-floor level which must surely have been used for hoisting material up to an upper-storey workshop. What is very much easier to distinguish is the outer show of the wealth of Lavenham. There are some quite magnificent houses, notably the Little Hall in the Market Place, which was originally an open hall house, centred on its principal room which would have been open from floor to rafters. There is some modern timber work introduced when the building was restored, but otherwise the main 'modernization' occurred when a jettied extension was added in the sixteenth century. Not quite so grand, but a splendid example of a clothier's town house of the sixteenth century is Molet House in Barn Street.

Although the wool industry vanished from Lavenham, the town did not simply slip back into a quiet existence as a country backwater. A new industry was introduced, the manufacture of that horsehair upholstery so beloved of the Victorians. New factories were built and a new name took over from Spryng: horsehair work was dominated by W W Roper and Sons. The principal factory can be seen just off the High Street, dominated by a white timber tower, but trade has long since ceased and the building has been converted into flats. The other obvious factory building is in Barn Street, and Lavenham is still showing its determination not to sink into mere picturesque quaintness. The factory has found a new use in pressing metal eyelets for anything from shoes to box files.

The new industry will not, however, give rise to the grand public buildings associated with the wool trade. The Guildhall was built for one of the medieval guilds, and is a superb example of the way in which timber was used as a necessary frame, but was designed also as a display of wealth. The sheer quantity of woodwork on show was intended to impress the passer-by with the notion that here was a building where nothing was skimped, no expense spared. The carving did little more than emphasize a point already made. But the most important building in terms of historical significance is the Wool Hall, originally another guildhall, but converted into the major merchants' trading centre for the town in the seventeenth century. It appears sumptuous, but already

The magnificent house that grew out of the simple Priory at Lavenham. The herb garden is set out in the form of a star, emblem of the de Veres, Earls of Oxford and the town's principal benefactors.

by that time the trade was in irreversible decline.

A day seems scarcely time enough to explore the town, and I am not going to attempt a detailed description of everything of interest in Lavenham – though I would recommend the town trail produced by the Suffolk Preservation Society. It is easy, however, to be so bowled over by the richness of the place that you lose sight of the story of development. It can help if you bring the focus down to just one point. I spent a morning at The Priory in Water Street. This is an astonishing building that was all but derelict when it was bought by its present owners, Alan and Gwenneth Casey in 1979. They spent four years on the basic restoration work, and they have not finished work yet. Their aim has been the highly commendable one of bringing back as many as possible of the original features, while still making a house which is clearly both a comfortable and a delightful place in which to live. So The Priory has that personal feeling that can be absent from even the best-run museum pieces. This personal sense comes in good measure from their decision not to be slaves to the past, so that their furniture, for example, is chosen to suit their tastes and yet remains entirely in keeping with the essential character of the house. Their own contribution to decoration lies mainly with the work of Ervin Bossanyi, who was no stranger to ancient buildings, for his stained glass can be seen in Canterbury Cathedral. But what makes the house so fascinating today is the way in which you can see the development brought about by centuries of change and growth. The exterior looks complicated, but the complexity seems even more apparent when you go inside.

The heart of the house is the great hall, which is not quite what it seems. This is the old hall of the priory, originally a simple two-bay house, which is just a way of saying that there are three vertical wooden frames, one at each end and one in the centre – as basic a structure as can be imagined. It was built in the thirteenth century and belonged to the Benedictine Priory of Earls Colne in Essex, which in turn was subservient to the abbey at Abingdon in the Thames valley. The endowment came from Alberic de Vere, related by marriage to William the Conqueror. His estate centred on Castle Hedingham included Lavenham. The town was already a place of some importance, so the endowment was a generous gesture. What the documents do not tell us is the use to which the hall was put. So things rested until the 1530s and the dissolution of the monasteries. The land and building that had been given by the de Veres were now sold back to them and the new owner was John de Vere, sixteenth Earl of Oxford. The plain hall of the monks was now transformed and passed to a local family, the Copingers. Henry Copinger, who bought it at the end of the sixteenth century, was great grandson of Thomas Spryng, the famous rich clothier. So the grandness of the house that we see today is a reflection of the richness of Lavenham at that time, where wealth could transform a simple house to something altogether grander.

What can we see of the original house today? The immediate answer would seem to be not a lot, for the old hall is no longer open to the rafters, and a splendid fireplace of richly coloured, hand-made Tudor bricks stands at one end where once smoke escaped through a gap in the roof. A new upper floor has been added, reached by an elaborate Jacobean staircase. But the view into one of the rooms added on later is through a little mullioned window, an odd feature to find inside a house. But this is because it once looked out on to the street, for it marks the outer wall of the original hall.

Every part of the house has its own story to tell of changing ideas on houses and how to make them livable. When the hall was extended, a solar was added on the upper floor. The addition of a kitchen brought with it a screened passage that led right through from front door to back. What was, in effect, an entirely new five-bay house was tacked on to the side of the old hall. Commerce appeared on the scene, and the merchant had his own chamber in which business could be conducted. There are stories to be seen in the detailing of all the various parts. In the kitchen you can see just how such a house was built by prefabrication. The timbers were all cut to size and joints carved out in the carpenter's workshop. Then it was all brought to the site for assembly. The various timbers had to be marked to make sure the right pieces came together, and the kitchen beams still show the original Roman numerals carved by the builders. The chamber at the top of the stairs was a principal bedroom, a place of comfort but also a room that was expected to look rather fine. The owners could have had it panelled in oak, and had the beams carved, but they took the cheaper way out. The walls were painted to resemble oak and the beams painted to give the impression of ornate carvings. In a house which had to be both living quarters and office, it was obviously an advantage to be able to shut work away. A two-way door stands by the merchant's room, which could close off the area for private discussions or be swung through 90 degrees to open the whole area up again. Wherever you look, there is a story of changing styles and changing use. Even the garden has its memories of the past with a splendid herb garden laid out in the design of the de Vere star. At the end of the visit, I felt that a walk round this one house told almost as much about the history of Lavenham as a walk round the entire town. And the blazing log fire in the huge fireplace was a comforting sight after the cold walks through the fens and the deluges on the Devil's Ditch.

ROADS, REBELLIONS, AND MASSACRE

Bridge of Orchy-Kinlochleven-Glencoe, 27 miles (43 km), OS maps 41, 50.

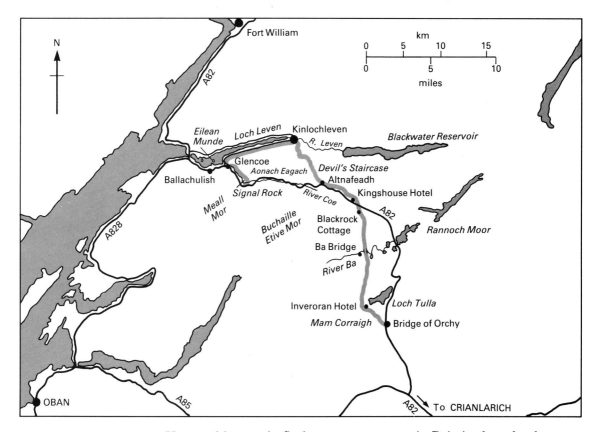

You could scarcely find a greater contrast in Britain than that between the fens and rich farmland of East Anglia and the moors and mountains of the Scottish Highlands. Yet great as the contrast is now, it was even more marked three centuries ago. The East Anglia we have just left was a settled, wealthy land with good transport by both land and water. The Highlands were primitive; a rough region where tribal loyalties fuelled a seemingly endless procession of bloody quarrels. Roads, quite simply, did not exist, though they were soon to appear – not in the first instance to promote trade and commerce, but to help bring peace to a troubled region. That sounds an admirable aim, but the peace was the King's Peace, and there was a distinct lack of agreement as to which head should carry the crown. Arguments on that issue were to dominate the region right up to the middle of the eighteenth century. It is against that roughly sketched-in background that this walk has to be seen.

My journey started at Bridge of Orchy, an insignificant point on most modern maps, easily missed by motorists racing up the A82, and no more than a minor halt on the railway from Glasgow to Fort William. Yet, geographically, this is a place of no little importance. The river valley coming up from the south provides what is virtually the only feasible transport route from Tyndrum up towards Fort William and the west coast – and at Loch Tulla, a road engineer must take a decision, either to follow a line to the east or to the west of the loch. The modern choice is the former, but my walk was to take me on the other route. And, to travel in that direction, the river must be crossed, hence Bridge of Orchy. The bridge itself was constructed about the year 1750, as part of a road-building programme designed quite specifically to help English troops keep the Highlands under control following the violent years of the Jacobite rebellions. The man in charge of developing a road system to move the soldiers through the rough mountain regions was General Wade. It was an undertaking that has been compared with the work of the Roman military engineers, a comparison which Wade himself was not inclined to discourage. The finest of his bridges, across the Tay at Aberfeldy, carries a plaque bearing just that message. The point was reinforced by having one plaque engraved in English, the other in Latin. The native Gaelic receives no place in the scheme, for the English were by then at pains to suppress all manifestations of Scottish

The Bridge of Orchy, built around the year 1750 as part of the military road to Fort William, constructed under the direction of General Wade.

national fervour. None of this is to be seen, however, at Bridge of Orchy, where the bridge itself is a plain, segmented arch of stone – handsome enough, but decidedly not gaudy. Its design is credited to one of Wade's officers, Major Edward Caulfield. Were the comparisons justifiable? Was the road through the Highlands comparable with, say, Akeman Street? The answers to those questions begin to emerge as you walk the old military road, but before setting out along that way I was to take a track that had existed long before the English troops moved in, and which now has a new life as part of the rapidly developing leisure uses of the Highlands.

Much of this walk follows the West Highland Way, yet another long-distance footpath, and the first section of 3 miles (5 km) follows a rough track that climbs over the shoulder of Mam Corraigh and then drops down to the Inveroran Hotel at the head of Loch Tulla. I had hoped for a fine day, for the sky the previous evening had been tinged with those pink and red streaks that are supposed to delight shepherds. I got the fine weather eventually but only after the morning had turned first grey, then black, and the rain had changed from a light drizzle to a drenching storm. Walking in the Highlands at least offers variety. The path winds up through a forestry plantation, a familiar part of the modern Scottish scene. It is often decried as a modern intrusion in the landscape, but this whole area was once covered by a large pine forest. The view from the top of the hill shows remnants, a few clumps of tall pine scattered around the edge of Loch Tulla. But before the loch is reached, there is, in damp weather – and with over 230 centimetres (90 inches) of rain a year, there is a good chance it will be damp – a peaty squelch to be undertaken. But although the ground may be wet, with standing pools of rich, reddish-brown water, there is not the same cloying effect that you get in a valley of heavy clays. At the end of the climb I was rewarded with a fine view over the loch, with its tree-studded islands. It presents a somewhat odd appearance for it seems to have no defined banks, but simply be a spreading-out of water over the land as though it was a temporary flood rather than a permanent feature. On the far bank stands a rather grand house, Black Mount. It represents one of the more recent developments in the life of the area – the arrival of the sporting gentleman who came in the nineteenth century to fish the streams for salmon and the loch for trout, and to shoot in the hills. But by the time of the sporting estates, the old crofting life was already slipping away into history.

The path headed downhill to the Inveroran Hotel, a replacement for an older inn that was once visited, and not greatly enjoyed, by Wordsworth. It was first a drovers' inn, a stopping place on the long

The Inveroran Hotel, once used by drovers taking their cattle to market, but which failed to win the approval of Wordsworth. It finds more favour with modern walkers and fishermen.

trek when the black cattle of the area were taken south to market. Before the arrival of General Wade, the drovers' road was the nearest thing to a recognized transport system in this area. It has left few physical marks behind, other than inns such as this and tracks which have memories of centuries of use. Cattle were a vital part of the Highland economy. They were raised here, widely traded and just as widely stolen. The land in this area has never been good, and the Macdonalds of Glencoe cast decidedly envious eyes over their better-endowed neighbours. The sixteenth and seventeenth centuries were a prime time for the reivers, the cattle raiders, and a favourite target was Glen Lyon, the home of the Campbells. Many of the cattle that came on the track past Loch Tulla came from the valley to the east and ended up hidden away in the secret valleys among the hills of Glencoe. It was, however, a dangerous trade and, after one expedition, thirty-six Macdonalds were hanged outside the Campbell castle of Meggernie.

The modern Inveroran Hotel continues a now lengthy tradition of catering for the fishermen and walkers who have taken the place of the old reivers and drovers, and a remarkably hospitable place it is too. Wordsworth would, no doubt, revise his poor opinion. Here, suitably refreshed, I could continue my route along the West Highland Way which now followed the old Wade military road. The first part, as far as Forest Lodge, is tarmacked, but the plain, stone bridges with their simple rubble arches topped by dressed coping stones are the originals

General Wade's road heading off towards the entrance to Glencoe. Some of the original stone-cobbled surface has survived on this section which, not unlike a Roman road, is raised up with drainage ditches at the side.

of two centuries ago. Here the surviving pines and firs of the old Caledonian Forest look down somewhat haughtily on the regulated rows of their newer neighbours. And here, too, the military road appears very much in its original condition. It comes as quite a shock to find a cobbled pathway stretching off towards the wilderness of Rannoch Moor, for it is surprisingly well preserved all the way to Ba Bridge.

The aims of the military engineers are easily seen: to keep as direct a route as possible, and to provide a surfaced, well-drained road through extremely difficult countryside. Here I was on the very edge of that vast wasteland of Rannoch Moor, dotted with innumerable small lakes and ponds, criss-crossed by rivers and streams, and offering little more solid matter underfoot than rough, tussocky grass and soft soggy peat. The engineers wisely kept clear of all that, preferring to hug the higher shoulders of the mountains to the west. So the road climbs steadily through over 180 metres (600 feet) to reach a summit over 300 metres (1000 feet) above sea level, before dropping down only to climb up again for another 150 metres (500 feet). The modern road, the A82, takes an only slightly more circuitous route to reach the entrance to the Pass of Glencoe, but reaches its highest point at that entrance, and avoids severe gradients. On any rational assessment of the two roads, the modern route has to be seen as more sensible and indicative of more sophisticated surveying techniques. But what of the military road itself? Here one has to say that time has tested it and found it well made. Any road that can survive the annual winter onslaughts of the Highlands must be declared soundly built. The builders did, however, enjoy certain obvious advantages. All along the roadway I could see mounds and hummocks that had been quarried away to provide good hard granite for the soldiers who provided the muscle power for road building. The surface consists of a pavement of rounded stones, with rough gulleys and drains at the sides. Mountain streams are either culverted under the road or crossed by simple stone bridges. As the torrential rain seeped into the surrounding moorland, the advantages of this well built, stony way were all too obvious.

The roadway descends towards the bridge across the river Ba, and the last traces of forestry plantation disappear and the sense of a lonely,

All that remains of the great forest that once covered the region are the twisted stumps of trees rising up from the treacly, black morass of a peat bog on the edge of Rannoch Moor.

desolate land now seemed to me to be absolute. It is not difficult to imagine the sense of dismay with which an English soldiery would enter such a region in the days before the road was built. To the east the lumpy wet landscape of Rannoch Moor spread dourly on; a land of brown, peaty pools and rough grass across which the rain was driving in great, grey wedges. It looked exactly what it is, an inhospitable, all but unuseable tract of land. To the west and north, the mountains rose up, their tops mainly obscured by clouds that sat stolidly on the summits or hung like dirty, unwashed net curtains over the faces of the crags. Yet even this is not quite the untouched landscape it appears. Once this was farming land, and I could see a ruined cottage sitting at the centre of a web of stone walls that marked out fields which had long since returned to nature. The old pattern of life began to change in the years after the Jacobite Rebellion of 1745. Landlords found that the local farmers seldom had any official rights of ownership over the land on which they lived and worked, and where their families had lived and worked for generations before them. The old way of life, keeping a few fields for crops, a flock of sheep, and a small herd of cattle began to give way to a new system. Sheep were no longer grazed for food but for wool to meet the growing demands of the new mills of an industrial world. The crofters were summarily expelled from their homes in the infamous Highland Clearances, which explains why there are more families of Scot's descent in the old areas of empire than there are in Scotland. The little farms collapsed into the ruins which are now almost the sole reminders of those earlier times.

Beyond Ba Bridge, the surface of the road deteriorated to become a rough track and only the culverts and the flat parapets of the bridges indicated that this was indeed still the line of the Wade road. The route took me high over the flank of Meall a Bhuirdh and down to the mouth of Glencoe. There are few more awe-inspiring sights in Britain than this dark valley, so closely shut in by mountains. On a day of wild rain and piled clouds, its mood seemed positively Wagnerian, and the scenery is not merely dramatic but seems almost to topple over into melodrama. Glencoe inevitably stirs memories of the infamous massacre, and the historical resonances add still darker and more melancholic chords to the main theme. We shall be returning to that story further along the way, but the very first glimpses of Glencoe also offer thoughts about the changing history of the region.

A solitary building stands by the way, Blackrock Cottage, a typical small croft, single storeyed with rough, whitewashed stone walls, and a roof tied down and weighted as protection from the wind. Today it marks the spot where the new industry of the area takes over – tourism.

A little way above it is a chairlift up the hillside, offering summer tourists a painless way to a mountain view and taking winter visitors to the busy ski slopes. And the heavy traffic on the nearby main road was a further reminder of the importance of holiday-makers to the region's economy.

Here I was on the margin between the high mountains and the wastes of Rannoch, and here it was the peat that revealed the story of a landscape that has changed. Twisted, bleached roots spread out above the dark-brown pools, survivors of the great forest that once covered the area. Across the main road was the Kingshouse Hotel, which was built at much the same time as the military road. By then, cattle rustling was virtually at an end, but the locals soon found a new profitable enterprise, and the inn became a favourite meeting place for salt smugglers. Here the old road again takes a higher line than the new, which at least brings the advantage that walkers are kept well clear of the cars and caravans.

It was here that I began my second day. Overnight the wind had risen and now darkly piled clouds sped across the hills which were viewed as in a peep show; now sullenly dark, now emerald bright as a shaft of sun gleamed on grass and heather. Then, as though a curtain had been twitched across the sky, the light went out again. Once more, the path ahead of me was tarmacked for part of the way because this section was, for a time, not only the military road but the start of a new road that was built in 1785 straight through the Pass. After that, walkers on the West Highland Way are directed on to a soggy track that meanders up and down the valley side. In the wetter spots, this track broadens as successive groups of walkers have tried to keep their feet dry. I was left wondering why everyone keeps so slavishly to the designated route, instead of striking out on their own. The most likely answer is that there is a certain comforting certainty about a recognized route: you know that you will not end up either in a bog or confronted by a dangerous precipice. And there are always those who take a special satisfaction in being able to announce that they have 'done' the West Highland Way. But these long-distance paths do, quite clearly, present problems of erosion as thousands of booted feet stomp across them each and every year.

The route proved to be somewhat wayward: climbing up the hillside and then dipping right back down to the main road. At Altnafeadh it reached one of the few remaining working farms in the glen, where ewes were being separated from their lambs with the help of an enthusiastic collie and to the accompaniment of much mournful bleating and baaing. The farmhouse itself was a snug affair, crouched behind a protective screen of trees. And it was here that the route changed direction. The

Two back-packing walkers toiling up the zigzag route of the Devil's Staircase. This section of the military road fell into disuse after the completion of a new road through Glencoe in 1785.

original military road turned off sharply to the north, following the steep track of an old, rough drove road over the hills to the valley of the Leven. At its best, it must have been a daunting route for an army and all its attendant baggage to take, so it comes as no surprise to discover that it was soon abandoned in favour of the new, gentler route down the middle of Glencoe itself. It remains, nonetheless, a wonderfully exhilarating route for walkers, not too arduous but offering magnificent views of the mountains and across Rannoch Moor. The whole scene was dominated by the shapely cone of Buchaille Etive Mor, which had just emerged from behind its veil of clouds. The path climbed steeply uphill, then became set into a series of zig-zags, designed to reduce the gradient, but adding a great deal to the distance walked. This track is known as the Devil's Staircase and it must certainly have seemed devilish to the unfortunate soldiers sent from England to build it. It must have seemed even worse to those who tramped up with full packs on their backs, sweating away under their heavy woollen uniforms. Its life as a military road may have been limited, but it had already achieved a place in history in its previous existence as a drove road. It was over this route that Lieutenant-Colonel Hamilton marched his troops in February 1692, arriving just too late to take any very real part in the Glencoe Massacre. It seems that no matter where you go in the vicinity of Glencoe, the events of that tragic day throw their long shadows across the scenery.

The top of the climb at 486 metres (1600 feet). is not only welcome because the uphill slog is at an end but also for the superb views to both north and south. Here it really did seem that I was alone in the mountains in a completely natural setting, untroubled by the works of humans. It was an illusion. The vast lake that stretched away to the west was no natural loch, but an artificial reservoir, and no-one who has travelled anywhere at all in the region needs to be a great detective to work out its function. Every town has its electricity showroom, and the roads are busy with distinctive vans – and the name on both is the same 'Hydro Electric'. But the knowledge that the glittering sheet of water is the result of human interference with the landscape really did nothing to diminish my delight in the natural world. The track I was following was still that laid down by General Wade's engineers, but 200 years of disuse, following the completion of the road through Glencoe, have seen a steady reversion to something very close to a rough mountain track. Just occasionally, as when the path appeared as a ledge carved out of the rocky hillside, was I reminded of the effort that once went into the construction of this route.

It is perhaps up here that an English town dweller, such as myself, begins to feel most strongly the historical gulf that separated the two peoples who met here in conflict. This is as wild a country as you can find in Britain and those who lived here before road construction began were, of necessity, members of a self-sufficient, inward-looking community. Local loyalties were of far greater importance than the affairs of kings and distant courts. The call to arms sent out by Bonnie Prince Charlie met a ready response for it came charged with all the appeals of tribal loyalties. It was a call back to tradition, a call to support an old, established order. Even now change seems to have little real meaning among the silences of the hills. Ranged against the Highlanders were the representatives of a new form of society, moving on to industrialization and more concerned with international affairs than local arguments. The result was inevitable, and the military road, however crude its construction, represented the imposition of the new age on to the old. The time of isolation was ended.

The conflict of which the Jacobite Rebellion was no more than a part was a conflict between two contrasting societies, and only incidentally between the dynasties of the Catholic Stuarts of Scotland and the Protestant Hanoverians. The real revolution was technological and social and we can all see the results. Nevertheless, many of us still find that the new prosperity is not, of itself, enough. So the hills in which the challenge to man was once the challenge of how to make a living in a harsh landscape, now offer a physical challenge to urban people who still feel a need to keep in touch with the natural world. In that sense, at least, the conflict epitomized by the tartans of the clans and the red coats of the soldiers has still not been completely resolved.

The route from the summit pass comes as an altogether delightful rough track that swoops down to bouldered streams where the water

A massive staircase of pipes carries water from a reservoir high in the hills to work the turbines that, in turn, produce electricity for the aluminium smelter in Kinlochleven.

boils among the rocks and climbs again to bring new arrangements of the mountain scene. For some 2 miles (3.2 km) from the summit of the Devil's Staircase, there was nothing to disturb the tranquillity, the sense of being quite alone in wild country. The change when it came seemed slight enough – nothing more than a small, square building behind which a small pond was being whipped by the wind into a frenzy of spray. But now the track broadened and, though still hardly of main-road standard and very steep, it was clearly used by motor vehicles. And, as I strode downhill, so the picture became clearer. The square building stands above a system of pipes that lead downhill towards the now visible buildings of Kinlochleven. At first, the scale of the enterprise scarcely registered, for the pipes seemed insignificant in the wide mountain scenery but, as I got nearer, the perspective changed. This turned out to be engineering on a monstrous scale. Water was thundering through those pipes, dropping down nearly 300 metres (1000 feet) from the reservoir to sea-level. My own first impression at the top of this giant water slide was of a mill pond, and so in a way it was. But instead of dropping water a short distance down on to a wheel that would power a few simple pieces of machinery, here the force was being used to turn massive turbines which would generate electricity to power a vast complex.

The road continued, steeply down through woodland, crossed a torrent of water on a tributary of the Leven and eventually arrived at Kinlochleven and the end of the pipe line. The river in the valley seemed a puny thing, which it inevitably was considering the quantity of water that had been dammed and diverted to provide power for the industrial works at the bottom. For here was the aluminium works for which all the efforts of the engineers were expended, where the hydro-electric power is put to work. It seems, and is, a long way from the life of the peaceful crofters, not to mention the bloodthirsty reivers. But once past the works, at least the Leven returns to something like its natural condition. The waters from the dam high up on the Blackwater reservoir, having completed their work are released to roar back to swell the river as it broadens out to feed Loch Leven.

At first sight, there seems very little of historical interest in Kinlochleven, which is much what you would expect in a place which did not exist at all until the beginning of this century. But it is a part of the Highland story nonetheless, for it represents one of the serious attempts made to revive the economic health of the area after the disasters of war and the tragedy of the clearances – even if it was not the first industry to reach the district. The hydro-electric scheme made use of the one element which is seldom in short supply in these mountains, water. The aluminium smelter that was to make use of that power was built between 1905 and 1909, and it was one of the great industrial marvels of the day. The choice of Kinlochleven was determined by one other major factor which always has to be taken into account when siting a new industry, the availability of transport. This site stands at the head of a navigable sea loch and you can still see the track bed of a 3-foot (0.9-metre) gauge electric railway that joined the works to the pier at the head of the loch. The new village for the workforce was built as a whole, planned and laid out in blocks which, though practical, can scarcely be described as beautiful. One does not feel encouraged to linger.

The West Highland Way now continues on, as does the military road, to Fort William, which was indeed once a fort and which was given several different names before settling for the present version after a major rebuilding during the reign of William III. It was one of the few strategic centres to hold out against the Jacobites in both the '15 and '45 rebellions. It was this that contributed to its importance and made it one of the main centres to which General Wade directed his road network. Of those days, however, there is now scarcely so much as a memory, for the fort itself was knocked down when the railway came to the Highlands. Fort William remains an important centre, but now for tourism, not defence. It is perhaps the ultimate irony that the most popular items on sale at the many gift shops are swathed in tartan – in the fort from which the law forbidding all displays of tartan was enforced two centuries ago. My path, however, now lay in a different direction, along the shore of Loch Leven and back towards Glencoe.

There is little space between the loch and the sharply rising hills to the south into which to fit a road but, fortunately for the walker, it is now remarkably peaceful with a minimum of traffic. This was not always so for, until recently, all the traffic between Glencoe and Fort William that did not take a short cut by ferry had to go all the way round the loch. The new bridge at Ballachulish solved that problem, so that only local traffic now appears down this way. Although the hills sweep practically down to the water's edge, there is little of that feeling of claustrophobia which can overcome travellers in Glencoe. Trees soften the hillside and hide the hard edges of the crags. Sheep graze by the lochside on what is, for this part of the world, remarkably lush grass. The farmers, however, have found other profitable uses for their land, and there were camping and caravan parks spread down both sides of the loch.

The most prominent feature that struck me as I approached Ballachullish was the bridge striding over the narrow inlet that divides Loch Leven from Loch Linnhe. There is, however, more to Ballachullish than this for, before the aluminium works were built, this was the major centre for employment in the whole region. Slate has been quarried here since the 1690s, and reached a peak of production in the last century, when more than 2000 men were employed. I turned off, however, just before Ballachullish for the village of Glencoe, but not without a foretaste of the main theme that lay ahead. Out in the loch was the island of Eilean Munde, where the ruined church marks the burial ground of the chiefs of the Macdonalds. It was rather more evocative in its way than the village of Glencoe itself, which consists largely of trim, neat, very suburban-looking houses. There is a Macdonald monument, erected in Victorian times, but there is none of that emotional pull which almost every visitor feels when they reach the glen itself. There is, however, an excellent small musuem, housed in one of the few remaining simple stone crofts of the area. It offers a wealth of information, compressed into an astonishingly small area and it was clearly founded as a labour of love. But my path was to carry me a little further yet, on into the deep ravine of the glen which seemed, to me at least, an altogether appropriate finale to the journey.

At the end of the village, the river Coe is crossed by a single-arched, hump-backed bridge, roughly contemporary with Wade's road. Here I left the houses behind as the road snaked off into a deep, wooded valley. This is not a view of Glencoe that the streams of visitors driving down the main road ever see. It is a peaceful valley, and the woodland at first is not a modern plantation, but a mixture of firs and deciduous trees, birch, oak, and rowan. And all the time as I walked, the busy little Coe provided a gently murmuring accompaniment. Gradually the view opened out to the north and the high rocky ridge of Aonach Eagach. But my route was pointed out to me by a gateway in the woods, where a sign was inscribed 'Signal Rock'. A pathway, softened by pine needles writhed through a dark, rocky conifer forest, which I felt would have made an ideal setting for an enactment of a story by the Brothers Grimm. But then I climbed out of the darkness of the trees to a rocky outcrop, from which I could look out over the mountains of Glencoe. This was Signal Rock, and it was here, according to tradition, that in the early hours of February 1692, a fire was lit to indicate that the Massacre of Glencoe should begin. The events that followed still seem to colour the way we all view this valley. There is scarcely a guide book nor tourist guide that fails to comment on the sense of doom that seems to hang over Glencoe. If one of the objectives of walking with a sense of history at the forefront of the mind is to try to capture the spirit and essence of a place, then one could say that here that end is achieved. But how much of what we feel is a direct result of observation, and how much an emotional response helped on its way by factors that have nothing to do with the slaughter of 1692?

First, and most often commented upon, is that sense of darkness that goes so aptly with grim events, but which is really little more than a natural response to a particular environment. The prevailing westerlies, bringing their load of water from the Atlantic, sweep down the glen and lift on the high peaks to form a pall of cloud. It makes for a somewhat gloomy scene, but the clouds would lower as dully over Glencoe if life here had remained impeccably peaceful and law abiding. So if one ignores the irrelevancies of climate, what messages can the landscape of Glencoe send back to us? To answer that question, the story of the events needs to be told and put into perspective.

There are two quite distinct and separate threads which meet and unite at Glencoe. The first represents the dynastic struggles for the throne of England and Scotland, between the last of the Stuarts, James II and William of the House of Orange, a struggle complicated by the religious affiliations of Catholics and Protestants. Then there was the local thread, the long history of years of feuding between the neighbouring clans of Campbells and Macdonalds. That these two threads were eventually to become entwined was an unhappy historical accident. The story begins with William of Orange's offer of a pardon to all those chiefs and their clans who swore allegiance to him by 1 January 1692. Alastair Macdonald had four months in which to comply, but he was an old man, set in his ways and loth to abandon ancient loyalties. He deferred until the very last moment his journey to take the oath of allegiance. On 30 December 1691 he set off for Fort William only to be told that the oath could only be administered at Inverary. Bad weather delayed him, and bureaucracy delayed him yet further. But the oath was duly taken, albeit five days late. That would scarcely have mattered if the Macdonalds had not acquired such a foul reputation as thieves, and brutal, not to say murderous, thieves at that. The delay was a marvellous opportunity for their enemies to seek revenge, and the Macdonald enemies were men of considerable power and even included William III himself among their number. The decision was taken to exterminate this troublesome clan – and this was not, it should be noted, a decision of their arch enemies, the Campbells. It was a decision that was sent for implementation to the professional soldiers of Fort William, Lieutenant-Colonel Hamilton and Major Duncanson. The orders were quite explicit: 'You are hereby ordered to fall upon the Rebells, the McDonalds of Glenco, and putt all to the Sword under seventy. You are to have a speciall care that the old fox and his sons doe upon no account escape.'

Such were the orders and it was either pure accident or English deviousness that the man given the responsibility of carrying them out was a Campbell. Captain Robert Campbell was a weak, somewhat pathetic figure – a bankrupt alcoholic, in no position to argue with his superiors. So the plot was laid, that would damn all Campbells, however innocent, as treacherous rogues, and picture all Macdonalds as innocent victims. For history remembers the name of Robert Campbell who obeyed orders and forgets those of Hamilton and Duncanson who issued them. And this is almost entirely due to another complicating factor, the Highland code of ethics, far stricter than any laws enacted by any Parliament.

Orders were duly issued, and Campbell marched his soldiers into Glencoe, where they asked for and received quarters and hospitality. No-one would describe the Highlands of the seventeenth century as places of high moral standards: theft and murder were virtually accepted as part of the pattern of life. One rule, however, was sacrosanct – guests were treated generously and, in return, the hospitality of hosts was never abused. The special horror of Glencoe stems from that, for it was Campbell's troops who were given the task of slaughtering their hosts. Yet, in the event, it was a wretched, bungled afffair. The order was given for the extermination to begin, yet the soldiers killed less than forty, while hundreds escaped to the mountains. Perhaps the Highland code of ethics worked on the troops after all. Or one could take the cynical view that the soldiers were simply incompetent and once the alarm was raised, the troops would have found themselves trying to cope with a difficult and positively hostile terrain. The latter view is certainly one that is reinforced when you look out from Signal Rock.

The valley of Glencoe is wild; the farms of three centuries ago were widely scattered and, before the construction of the military roads, communications were extremely difficult. There was no shortage of

*Signal Rock, Glencoe.
According to tradition, it was
on this rock that a fire was lit
on a winter's morning in 1692
to indicate that the Massacre
of Glencoe should begin.*

avenues of escape from the glen. Having said that, however, it would
seem likely that the families roused from their beds and forced to flee in
the depths of a Highland winter were scarcely better placed than those
who stayed to face the muskets and swords of the soldiers. Look out
from Signal Rock and you can see that wildness and picture the
hardship of the families who made their escape across hills such as Meall
Mor, rising sternly up to the south. But you can also understand the
problems faced by soldiers, totally unused to this rugged mountain
scenery. In the event, the massacre can best be described as a misguided
shambles. The fox's sons did escape, far more Macdonalds survived
than perished, and poor old pathetic, drunken Captain Robert
Campbell carried the blame for obeying the orders handed down by his
superiors. It is doubtful if any military operation could have succeeded
in such a region against locals who knew the terrain intimately. Yet the
memories linger, and no-one can stand on Signal Rock and stare out
over the valley, its enclosing crags and heathered slopes, or watch the
dark clouds massing to advance over the peaks, and quite forget the
events of 1692.

   If you want a walk to end climactically, then Signal Rock is the place
to end. But in practice, of course, you have to move on, back to
civilization, back to a comfortable bed, a hot meal and, this being
Scotland, a comforting nightcap dram. So I walked on to the Clachaig
Inn. Down below on the main road was the Visitor Centre, catering for
the passing tourist wanting a quick run-down on the area. The hotel
walls, however, are covered by photographs of climbers scaling the
nearby cliffs. Together they represent the new Glencoe; no longer the
home base of a feudal clan, but an area where visitors outnumber the
residents many times over. The past is remembered, after a fashion, but
now the old, deep, bitter emnities are reduced to a jokey sign in the bar:
'No Hawkers or Campbells'.

THE INDUSTRIAL LANDSCAPE

Sowerby Bridge to Manchester, 33 miles (53 km), OS maps 103, 104, 109.

The canal basin at Sowerby Bridge, where the warehouses once held goods waiting trans-shipment between the Rochdale Canal and the Calder and Hebble Navigation. Today, the basin accommodates the new canal industry: holiday boats for hire.

The Industrial Revolution of the late eighteenth century marks one of the great turning points, not just in the history of Britain, but in that of the whole world. Its characteristics were the movement of manufacture from home to factory, new sources of power and new transport systems to move the raw materials and products of industry. The canals provided the first real innovations in British transport since the time of the Romans – literally thousands of miles of artificial waterway were constructed in the years between 1760 and the arrival of the railway age in the 1820s. I have chosen the towpath of the Rochdale Canal for this walk, because it served two of the greatest industries of the eighteenth and nineteenth centuries. It begins among the woollen mills of Yorkshire and ends in a spectacular plunge through the mills and

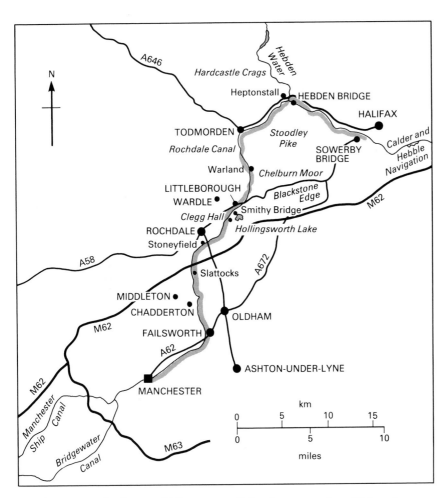

warehouses at the heart of 'Cottonopolis' – the great city of Manchester. There was another reason for this selection. These walks are all intended to be enjoyed as walks and I am well aware that not everyone shares my prediliction for walking beside greasy, oily water where little floats apart from plastic sheets, and the nearest you get to a movable object is an abandoned supermarket trolley. Even were I to hold out the prospect of seeing some historically important buildings along the way, I doubt if I should persuade many to follow my footsteps. The Rochdale Canal, however, is a trans-Pennine route which offers the superb scenery of hill and moorland to add to the interest of mill and factory.

As the towpath of the Rochdale Canal will form the path for virtually the entire journey, it might be as well to have some details of this, my constant companion. There are endless academic articles arguing over when the canal age began, but suffice to say that, by the 1760s, the principal elements were assembled – artificial waterways had been dug, taking a line independent of any natural river or stream; locks and aqueducts had been constructed, and the first tunnel had been begun. In 1770, an Act of Parliament authorized the construction of a trans-Pennine waterway to join the cities of Leeds and Liverpool. It was plagued with difficulties, mostly due to shortage of money, and work stopped altogether in 1777 and was not resumed until 1790. The 1790s, however, were the canal mania years. In the first five years of the decade, no fewer than forty-nine new canals were authorized, the Rochdale among them. Promoters had looked at the snail-like progress of the Leeds and Liverpool and had decided to put through an alternative plan of their own. They were not immediately successful. The line of the canal was first laid out by the engineer John Rennie who presented his plans to Parliament in 1792 and 1793, but was turned down largely because of the opposition of mill owners who feared that the canal would divert water from their concerns. Then in 1794, a second engineer, William Jessop, was brought in, and he produced new plans which allayed the worries of the industrialists; we shall see his solution to the problems of water supply along the way. The plan was approved and work began which was to end with the grand opening in December 1804. It was a very successful canal which, at its peak, was carrying half-a-million tons of cargo a year, which would have meant that anything up to 100 boats would have been working along the canal on any one day. It is also something of an oddity in that it was not nationalized along with the majority of the other canals in 1947. It is still the property of the Rochdale Canal Company and, although it fell derelict, it is currently being restored – not to carry coal, wool, and cotton but to take the new canal trade of pleasure boats.

I began my walk at Sowerby Bridge where the Rochdale Canal joins the Calder and Hebble Navigation. The latter represents an earlier stage of canal development in which rivers were made navigable by the construction of cuttings and locks. A junction is always an important place on a canal for, as each canal company was privately owned, so each had its own rate of charges for carrying cargo and, quite often, each had its own fleet of vessels. Here the junction was even more significant, for the Rochdale could accommodate vessels up to 22.5 metres (74 feet) long while the Calder and Hebble could only take vessels 17.5 metres (57 feet 6 inches long). So the most obvious feature is a range of warehouses where goods could be stored while waiting trans-shipment from one type of craft to another. A good deal of restoration work has gone on, and was still going on, here, and this is a very good example of distinctive canal architecture. Much has changed since I first came here, but what is still plain is the way in which the buildings were designed for a specific use. They have conventional wide doors on the land side for waggons to load and unload, but they also have arches over the water, so that boats could float underneath the building, for easy loading and to keep cargo under cover. Now the basin is home to a hire boat fleet.

At Sowerby Bridge I met the first of the thirty-six locks that would lift the canal to its summit among the Pennine Hills. These are big locks, capable of holding vessels of 22.5-metre (74-foot) length and 4.25-metre (14-foot) beam, or they can take two traditional canal narrow boats, side by side. In fact, they are rather more complex than they appear at first sight. One of Jessop's main concerns was to save water. Now every time a boat goes through a lock it drains out a lot of water which is released into the next length of canal, or pound, but which will eventually leave the canal altogether. An average lock full of water represents around 250 000 litres (55 000 gallons) – and that same amount is used whether you have a tiny rowing boat or a full-sized barge. Calder and Hebble barges would not need a 22.5-metre (74 foot) lock, so a lot of water would be wasted. Jessop designed his locks with an extra set of gates, so that it was possible to enclose a shorter section, just enough in fact to take Calder and Hebble vessels, a saving of some 54 545 litres (12 000 gallons). You can still see the recesses in the locks where the extra gates were fixed. He also planned his locks so as to keep the fall uniform throughout the whole system, so that when a lock was emptied at the summit it would pass down just enough water to fill the next lock and so on all the way down.

The start of the canal proper seems almost aggressively urban as it threads between houses, mills, and warehouses, but it was very disconcerting to find that I had scarcely begun my canal walk before the canal itself totally disappeared from view. All but a short section in Manchester was finally closed in 1952 so local authorities felt no need to accommodate the canal in later road-improvement schemes. Consequently, what had been a bridge over a waterway became a road over a water pipe, presenting an interesting challenge to would-be restorers. It re-emerged across the main road and, as it headed out into the country, the major themes of the journey announced themselves. For a start, the line the canal takes is clearly determined by the contours of the river valley. So, we have the canal taking the easiest route and attracting to itself its own kinds of development, particularly warehouses. The river, too, has its own pattern of development for although it is too shallow to take boats, it has quite enough fast-flowing

Patterns in stone: the irregular blocks of dry-stone walling contrast with the shaped stones of a bridge abutment, while the steps up from the canal have been worn into gentle curves by generations of users.

A hill stream draining down into the canal. The trough beside the bridge acts as a settling tank, so that sediment is not carried over into the canal.

water to provide power. So it is here that one finds early industrial development based on the water wheel. Canal for transport, river for power – that was the formula for success in the eighteenth century.

The shapes made by the land determined where the canal had to go, and the stone available beneath the surface provided the raw material for construction. Stone provides coping for the canal edge and for boundary walls; it is used for bridges and cottages – stone provides the dominant visual theme, not just on the canal but throughout the landscape. As I walked, I came to cuttings where the stone had been blasted away to make a route for the new waterway, and that same stone then reappeared in the canal structures. This makes for a satisfying unity between natural landscape and artificial waterway. It would become tedious if I were to list the details of every lock and bridge along the way, so I shall squeeze a lot of these descriptions together into the first part of the walk, from Sowerby Bridge to Hebden Bridge.

Firstly, and most importantly, come the locks, the watery staircase that was gradually lifting the canal up to the hills. The details here are always of interest. I particularly liked the way in which stone setts had been used to pave the overspill weir, over which water can flow round a lock. I also enjoyed the patterns cut through the years into bollards, as generations of boatmen had passed their ropes round the stone blocks. Simplicity is the key note, as seen in the square timber baulks used to make the plainest of footbridges. Even when disused, the workings of the lock are easily seen. The most obvious features are the robust iron paddle gears, simple ratchets that can be wound up by a windlass. At the drained locks, awaiting restoration, the way they work can be easily seen. A stone culvert leads from an opening in the wall below the waterline just outside the lock and then runs down to the bottom of the lock. The opening can be closed off by a paddle, moved up and down by the paddle gear. Raise the paddle and water will flow into the lock; close it and the flow stops. A similar device at the other end drains the lock. The fact that I was walking 'a towpath' was a reminder that, when the canal was built, the only source of power to pull the boat was a horse. This is all very well but imagine yourself approaching a lock. The horse stops but the boat sails cheerfully on its way. Bent iron rods at the lockside provided the brakes, the boatman slipping a line over as he went by to bring his boat to a halt.

Everywhere along the canal, I was particularly struck by the craftsmanship of the stone work, seen in the neat bridges as well as in simple mile posts carved with the intials R.C. or R.C.Co. Structures near the locks have their own messages about the working life of the canal. Looking at the many streams coursing down the hillside above the canal, it might seem that water supply would be a problem that could easily be solved. But natural streams carry dirt and grit with their water, which would silt up the still waters of the canal. So water from streams falls first into a stone trough where all the rubbish can settle out, while only the clean water will fall into the canal itself.

Once it was completed, the canal began to attract development to its banks. Mills and warehouses can be seen, usually across the water from the towpath, so that boats could draw up right alongside the wall for easy loading. Developments such as these need people so, along with the industrial buildings, you find new housing developments for the workers, some appearing as terraces set back from the water, others built right up to the water's edge. Ribbon development is not, after all, an invention of the twentieth century and the motor age.

There was more to the walk, however, than a minute examination of the canal environment. The geography of the region that relegated the canal to the valley bottom, also dictated the routes for road and railway engineers. They, too, had to find a space within the narrow valley confines. Transport routes form the axes for the industrial life of the area, but look away from them and a different pattern emerges, This is also the land of the hill farmer, of fields marked out by dry stone walls, where sheep are penned for grazing. Just as the canal buildings grew from the land, so too did the old farms – solidly built of local stone, many of them showing the traditional stone-mullioned windows of the South Pennines. This is a landscape which predates the industrial revolution, yet which seems to have survived it intact.

Houses for the workers who came to the new industries attracted to the canal were themselves built with walls falling sheer to the water.

Along the way, I came upon isolated mill buildings, some with the give-away chimney stack that shows they had moved out of the era of water power and into the steam age. This part of the story was seen at its clearest as I walked on towards Hebden Bridge. Up ahead, a hill rose up, topped by a church tower, and there was a distant prospect of open moorland over which vague tracks wandered. But, nearer at hand, the buildings were closing in, as the tall chimneys of steam-powered mills rose above the water. There is even a survivor from another industry which once played an important part in the life of the mill workers. A clog factory is still at work, though now they are more concerned with fashionable taste than the need for stout, industrial footwear. It is unfortunate that, although there is always a form of logic at work in the development of the landscape, it does not show itself in neatly arranged chronological order. But for those who would appreciate a history of the industrial revolution in miniature, I would recommend a walk through Hebden Bridge, though you must be patient for a while until the starting point of the story is reached.

Turn off the canal and follow the line of the river that comes in from the north, Hebden Water. In the centre of the town, the river is crossed by a high arched bridge with low parapets. This is a distinctive feature of this landscape, a packhorse bridge. In the days before the canal was built, the packhorse was the principal form of transport. Long trains of the animals were led across the hills from village and farm to market and back again. The high arch of the bridge was no obstacle to these sturdy beasts and the low parapet provided clearance for the packs slung across their saddles. From this bridge, a cobbled path leads steeply up the hillside to the village of Heptonstall. It is a delight, a clenched fist of a village, where farms and houses cluster together for comfort against the harsh Pennine winter. Here there are ample signs of former prosperity: a seventeenth-century grammar school and a sixteenth-century cloth hall, not so grand as that at Lavenham but by no means insignificant. And, again in echo of the Lavenham walk, a churchyard with two churches – though here the explanation is a simple one, for the first church was damaged beyond repair by a storm in 1847. Village piety is further marked by the splendid octagonal chapel whose foundation was laid in 1764 by John Wesley in person. And everywhere there is evidence of the source of Heptonstall's wealth in the weavers' cottages with their characteristic long windows on the upper floors which shed light on the looms. This is the old world of the cloth trade, of handloom and spinning wheel, and transport by pack animals, but look down on Hebden Bridge and you can see the new world that took its place.

In the late eighteenth century, Richard Arkwright established the

The new generation of steam-powered mills were built alongside the canal at Hebden Bridge to take advantage of cheap transport for coal and raw materials.

first water-powered cotton mill at Cromford in Derbyshire. Instead of the lone spinner at the cottage door, there were a thousand spindles turned by the water wheel. Emphasis moved from the hilltop village to the river in the valley. A new town grew up as mills spread down the length of Hebden Water. You can see them there still. Soon mechanical weaving was added to mechanized spinning, and the single-storey weaving sheds with their saw-toothed roofs set with north-facing lights appeared alongside the square, squat bulks of the spinning mills. Then water power gave way to steam power, and the canal came into its own, bringing in coal and raw materials for the mills. It also provided water, for the Act of Parliament allowed owners of steam engines within 20 yards (18 metres) of the canal to draw out water. But with all this new development crowding on to the valley floor, where were the people to

*Houses and mills crowd
together into the narrow valley
of the Hebden Water. The
saw-tooth pattern of the roof is
typical of weaving sheds,
where north-facing roof lights
provide even illumination for
the looms below.*

go? The answer can be seen in the extraordinary terraces clinging to the
hillside. Where, in other towns, houses were built back to back, here the
steep slope made this impossible. So houses were placed top to bottom
instead. On the upper side of the slope you see a conventional two-storey
terrace, but turn the corner and look at the other side and you see four
storeys, the bottom house having an entrance on the lower street.
Heptonstall represents the old way of life where cloth making was still
closely tied to farm and country: Hebden Bridge is the new age of close-
packed towns and steam mills. It was these new towns that the canal was
built to serve.

The next few miles of the walk presented me with some quite superb
scenery, and a chance to appreciate the problems faced by the canal
builders of the eighteenth century. The river valley narrows down to a
deep cleft struck through the Pennine hills. To the south, the hillside
climbs steeply to a crag-topped summit, and it was on this slope,
between hill and river, that the canal had to make its way. Any engineer
faced with such a task would feel a trifle daunted, but it must have
seemed exceptionally difficult two centuries ago when virtually nothing
in the form of mechanical aids was available. Pick, shovel, and
wheelbarrow were the tools of the canal builders, with the addition of
hand drills and black powder for blasting away the rocks. The men
whose muscle power built the waterways began their work on the early
navigations, such as the Calder and Hebble, which earned them the
name 'navigator', later abbreviated to the familiar 'navvy'. It is hard now
to imagine the impact they must have had on such a region, where the
village of Heptonstall was the major centre of population and Hebden

Bridge scarcely existed. Into this peaceful landscape came an army of itinerant workers; hard, rough men with a reputation – not entirely unjustified – for hard, rough living. These were the men who built what we now see. They levered out the stones to support the river bank, carved a ledge for the towpath, and dug out the channel for the new waterway. It was estimated that an experienced navvy could dig out 12 cubic yards (9 cubic metres) of earth a day – and if that does not sound a lot then ask any weekend gardener how long he would expect to take to dig a trench 1 yard wide, 1 yard deep, and 12 yards long (1 metre by 1 metre by 9 metres). I doubt if his answer would be one day. And even then the work was not complete, for the canal had to be made watertight. A mixture of sand or gravel, clay, and water was laid on the bed of the canal and stomped into place by heavy booted navvies. Once the canal was complete, it still needed to be maintained and the old maintenance yard is still there, with the remains of one of the old wide-beamed barges.

In spite of all the individual touches of historic interest met along the way, it was hard not to be distracted by the scenery. On one side were the woods and on the other the view to the hills. Looking back towards Heptonstall I could see the black cliffs of Hardcastle Crags while, up ahead, an obelisk marked the summit of Stoodley Pike beside the Pennine Way. But, if you come this way in summer you might be brought back to the historic theme by the clop of a horse's hooves on the towpath, as Calder Valley Cruising's horse-drawn narrowboat, *Sarah Siddons*, appears with its sight-seeing passengers. Why Sarah Siddons? Well, the boat began its working life on the Brecon and Abergavenny Canal, and Sarah Siddons was one of Brecon's more illustrious daughters.

At Todmorden, the canal passes right through the centre of the town, where the main road is carried over the water on an iron bridge. Beyond the bridge there is an absolutely fascinating area. That this was once a busy canal spot is plain from the cobbled towpath, the mills, and the warehouse with its still-prominent gantry crane. A flight of locks carries the canal up between the buildings, but nothing the waterway can offer can match the adjoining railway for dramatic impact. It rises high above the town on an embankment which falls sheer to the canal as a vast, curving brick wall. And where that ends, the lines cross the water on a viaduct decked out with castellated towers like the bastions of some medieval fortress. Quite what there was in nineteenth-century Todmorden to remind the engineers of the Lancashire and Yorkshire Railway of castles and knights in armour is a mystery, but there it is in all its splendour, complete with stone shields and arrow slits. It is

The giant, castellated viaduct built by the Lancashire and Yorkshire Railway quite dominates the locks of the earlier canals at Todmorden. There is clearly no water-shortage here, for the locks are overflowing.

Victorian engineering Gothic at its most delightfully absurd.

While the railway still carried its regular service of trains, the canal now came to an abrupt halt, just one of the many places where a bridge has been demolished and the roadway levelled out to ease the way for motorists and provide a headache for restorers. A few years ago, no one could see a future for the Rochdale Canal, so why preserve a bridge under which no boats would ever pass? What was not envisaged was the huge expansion in pleasure boating. But times do change. They have changed, too, for the textile industry, and this part of the walk brought a plethora of sturdy, well-proportioned stone buildings which one assumes will never again resound to the clatter of shuttles and the whirr of spindles. I found one solution at this same spot, conversion into housing. With its stone walls cleaned, the old mill positively sparkled, while the former engine house made another separate home. Further along was another small group of houses which have now also become historical rarities; prefabs, simple houses that came packaged for quick assembly to help fill the gaps left by German bombs. Protection from those same bombs was provided by Anderson shelters, now finding a new use as garden sheds. They are, in their own way, poignant reminders of a violent period in British history. A somewhat older, but equally distinctive, style of house could be seen just beyond Warland, where the Calderbrook and Rochdale roads meet. It is a lonely, octagonal building and was undoubtedly a toll house where travellers on the new turnpike road would have paid for the privilege of using the improved system. This is Steanor Bottom Bar toll house built around 1825, and it still displays a board giving the list of charges. Its odd shape enabled the toll collector to keep a look out in all directions, to make sure that no-one got a free passage.

Between Todmorden and Littleborough, the canal reaches its summit, marked by a little white lock cottage. Thirty-six locks had been needed to raise the waterway to this point – and, after only three-quarters-of-a-mile (1.2 km), the arrival of West Summit Lock announces the start of the descent down to the other side of the Pennines into Lancashire. Here you can see how the basic problem of water supply was solved. Feeders can be seen carved in the hillside, bringing the supplies to keep the canal topped up. They lead from reservoirs which are, in their own way, just as remarkable as the canal they serve. There are small reservoirs near the line of the canal on Chelburn Moor, another, much larger, at Blackstone Edge, over a mile (1.6 km) away, and, largest of all, Hollingsworth Lake near Littleborough. The latter actually became a popular holiday resort in Victorian times – a miniature inland sea for the inhabitants of Rochdale. In Rennie's original plans, the summit was to have been pierced by a tunnel, but Jessop preferred more locks and a deep, open cutting. Alongside, you can see how the neighbouring railway preferred the alternative solution. In digging tunnels, it was usual to work in from the ends, but also to sink shafts down to the correct line and work upwards from these, the material dug out of the tunnels being piled up as spoil heaps. The shafts were then left open for ventilation. They are still clearly visible as stumpy, open-topped brick towers on the hillside, occasionally emitting exhaust fumes as a train passes down below. The tunnel is dignified by the coat of arms of the Lancashire and Yorkshire Railway carved in stone over the southern entrance. One could take an interesting walk from this spot to see how different generations of transport engineers have tackled the problem of the hills, for just south of the Blackstone Edge reservoir, one can find an extraordinarily well-preserved section of Roman road.

Up ahead, the spire of Littleborough church marked not just the arrival of the next town, but also a change in mood and style. It signalled the end of the Pennines, an end to hills and millstone grit and the arrival of the flat lands under which lies coal – coal that was to form a major part of the cargo carried on the canal. The change is not abrupt, but is nevertheless very distinctly made in the space of the few miles that separate Littleborough from Rochdale. Littleborough itself seems very

The thirty-sixth lock from Sowerby Bridge has finally brought the canal to its summit, beneath the gritstone crags of the Pennines.

similar to Todmorden and the other Pennine towns but, when I turned back to look along the way I had come, I could see the hills rising steeply behind me, while up ahead, on a clear day, the only dominant features in a flat land were the distant tower blocks. Those who, like me, enjoy the hills must breathe a sigh of regret that that stage of the journey is over, though the memory of the stony hills lingers for a while. At Smithy Bridge, there is a reminder of the days when farmers mixed everything into their working lives. In one continuous building, there is a barn with its wide-arched waggon entrance, a conventional farmhouse and, at the end, a weaver's window marks where the farmer supplemented his income in the cloth trade. An even grander example of disparate factors coming together could be seen a little further on at Clegg Hall. The hall itself is a grand, if somewhat stern and now sadly decaying building. Its dark stone walls look down over the canal and its gabled front and mullioned windows speak of former prosperity. It is hemmed in now between a short terrace of weavers' cottages, as sadly neglected as the hall, and a mill, still at work.

The railway and canal now run side by side, both in deep cuttings. Here I could see the paucity of building stone, now reduced to a thin layer squeezed between crumbling shale. There was also a boundary stone, which I thought might be just another Rochdale Canal Company mark of ownership, but which turned out to belong to the nextdoor neighbour instead, for it was carved with the initials LYR. This glimpse of poor stone in the cutting prepared me for what lay ahead –

farmhouses built on timber frames. When I saw these I knew that the change in the environment was complete. But even more dramatic evidence began to appear with the mills of the valley. Once again, stone had disappeared, and in its place came a violently coloured red brick. This was Accrington brick, which came into favour for mill building at the very end of the nineteenth century. These giant, multistoreyed spinning mills differ from their predecessors not just in size, but also in style and use. Only rarely do you find weaving sheds alongside the spinning house, and these mills were built to take advantage of a new brand of faster, more efficient spinning machine, the ring frame. But the power source was still the mighty steam engine, and the engine houses with their tall windows were often the most highly decorated part of the new complexes. There was an obvious pride, too, in ownership, with names picked out in yellow brick, either on the water tower or less frequently on the tall mill chimney. These mills are the symbols of the mighty Lancashire cotton industry at the height of its prosperity, when this one small area was providing two-thirds of the world's manufactured cotton. Those were the years when the proud saying was that 'Britain's prosperity hung on a Lancashire thread'. No more: many of the mills are boarded up, others split into small units and converted to other uses. Cotton manufacture has now spread throughout the world, but Lancashire still keeps going even though its share of the world market is only a fraction of what it was. However, all is not gloom, and there is even a comparatively modern factory by the canal on the approach to Rochdale – Comfy Quilts and Textiles, still it seems hard at work.

One thing you might expect on the Rochdale Canal is that you would reach Rochdale – but you do not. The canal skirts round the southern boundary, though there was once an arm leading in towards the town centre through the district of Stoneyfield. I was not surprised to find the canal bordered by mills in ever greater concentrations, but I was rather sad at missing the centre of Rochdale. It boasts a splendid town hall, proclaiming civic pride on the grand scale, and a little shop where the Rochdale Pioneers began the Co-operative movement. But if Littleborough marked the end of the Pennine section, then Rochdale virtually marked the end of country walking. There are patches of green ahead, but increasingly the landscape would be dominated by the urban areas spreading relentlessly out from Oldham and Manchester. Those on the hunt for the picturesque will find little enough of it here. Yet to ignore it would be to miss the whole point of the Rochdale Canal. The waterways of the pre-railway age were the arteries which fed the raw materials that brought life to the growing industrial body. Without

The canal comes to an abrupt end in reedy shallows, its progress brought to a halt by the M62 which cuts directly across its path.

them that great period of industrial expansion would have been delayed for half a century. There is no point in complaining about the lack of attractive scenery, for the canal builders' ambition was to help cover the landscape with wealth-creating mills and factories. Whether we like or dislike the end result is a matter or personal taste, but this is the historical reality behind the lovely canal that will, one hopes, soon be busy with pleasure boats.

Restoration work has in fact continued to the south of Rochdale, but there it meets the most formidable barrier so far. Beyond a neat lock, new gates recently hung, the canal stopped and ahead six lanes of traffic charged along. The M62 has been dropped down straight on to the old canal. A short detour brought me to a path under the motorway and a farm literally metres away from the thunderous traffic. The old confronts the new, for the farm looks back to an earlier age, with its stone-mullioned windows strongly reminiscent of the style of the Pennine hill farms. There was a return, too, to green fields even if the signs of urbanity were never very far away. The land had none of the obvious rise and fall of the hill sections, but I was still going steadily downhill dropping through a flight of six locks at Slattocks, one of the few flights with a lock cottage, easily recognized as such by its position, face turned towards the canal not the road. Such cottages usually appear with rather more frequency on canals. They were homes to the lock-keepers and lengthmen, who would have been responsible for a particular section of waterway, in which a flight of locks would have been the most important feature.

Walking along, I could see how the immediate canal environment predates the spread of the towns. The old materials were still used, with stone predominating. There was a particularly lovely stretch just before the canal made a great U bend round the valley to the north of Chadderton. Everything was superbly well done, no detail out of place, from the dressed stone blocks of the lock walls to the graceful arch across the overspill weir. But the canals, and their successors the railways, made the transport of materials cheaper and easier. Builders no longer had to rely on what was available locally, so expensive stone gave way to cheap, mass-produced bricks. You can see how the railway engineers themselves turned to the new material, as the line crosses the canal on a brick bridge. The bridge itself is notable for being built on the skew, not crossing the canal at a right angle. This technique was pioneered on canals such as the Rochdale, and it is fascinating to see the curious pattern of slanting brickwork needed to produce such an arch.

Chadderton marks one edge of the great Oldham complex, a centre famous not merely for its mills but also for the manufacture of mill machinery. The tall mill chimneys and the stark, squat blocks below them are such familiar landmarks that one can easily forget that someone had to make the machinery to go in them. One of the most famous of them all was to be found in Oldham, Platt Brothers, where everything was done from the initial casting of iron parts to final assembly: they even had their own collieries to provide fuel for the furnaces. From here, machines went round the world and I have seen their name cast into looms and spinning machines as far apart as America and India. There are still working foundries down by the canal, most easily recognized by the piles of casting boxes in the yards. These are square, open boxes into which a pattern is placed and then packed round with sand. When the pattern is removed, the space left is filled with molten metal to form the casting.

Ahead, tower blocks vied with chimneys for the domination of the horizon as the open spaces got fewer. The authorities were faced with a dilemma when the canal closed. A derelict canal can deteriorate in no time at all into an evil-smelling ditch of stagnant water into which any and every variety of rubbish can be dumped. A working canal is a living canal, the movement of boats helps to keep the channel scoured and the constant use of locks keeps fresh water running through the system. A used canal simply cannot be allowed to deteriorate into a rubbish dump, or boats will not get through. That option, however, was discarded in favour of what officialdom had dubbed 'a linear water park'. In place of locks, a series of low weirs was built, to form a gentle cascade. The area along the canal was made into a walkway, trees were planted, and at various points, objects of sculptural significance were set into the water.

It won a civic award. I doubt if it would win one now. The linear water park has become a linear rubbish dump and the sculptures extol, in fairly equal measure, the virtues of Manchester's football clubs and various forms of carnal activity. The water is, however, popular with small children who paddle in welly boots, net tiddlers or ride their bikes through the water in pursuit of loudly complaining ducks.

If, however, a working canal seems a better option than the present system, then there is at least one more truly daunting obstacle to be overcome before it can be achieved. In Failsworth, the canal does one of its temporary disappearing acts, but this time it is not just a question of a lowered bridge – a whole new supermarket now stands where the boats, nostalgically recorded on a nearby pub sign, once floated. The remaining problems met along the way seem quite insignificant by comparison. I had to make occasional diversions, as the buildings closed in ever tighter on the approach to Manchester. But with the arrival at the city centre, the whole character of the canal changes yet again. The turning point arrived at Ducie Street junction, where the Rochdale Canal meets the Ashton. For a short distance at least, the Rochdale was joined in to the whole system of British navigable waterways, for the Ashton links in with the main canal system of the Midlands, while the Rochdale itself finally appears if only for a mile-and-a-half (2.4 km), as a useable waterway. It is a short stretch to be sure, but it is packed with interest and made a most fitting climax to the walk.

There are indications of the special nature of this final stretch even before it arrives. This is the commercial heart of the mighty cotton empire that dominated the world scene well into the present century. Street names speak of international connections – Bengal Street appears, China Street follows, and so it goes on. The message is also clear in the buildings that line the route as it takes a final plunge down through the heart of the city through the last nine locks. Once, the beginning of this stretch was marked in the grand manner at Ducie Street, where the Rochdale Canal Company still has its offices. There were immense warehouses here, six storeys high, grim bastions that lowered over the canal. They have gone and, in their place, is a car park. But if the old importance of the canal has died away, the land surrounding it is still part of the city centre and represents valuable real estate – the junction is no more than a couple of hundred metres from Piccadilly station. So, predictably, the canal does one of its now-familiar disappearing acts, vanishing from sight beneath a tall office block. This time, however, the waterway has not been blocked off, for the building rises on concrete stilts and there in the gloom is a working lock. Boats

come down here while over their heads typists type and executives make executive decisions. It is one of the strangest spots on the whole of Britain's canal system.

Beyond the Piccadilly tower block, the canal passes through an urban canyon. On every hand there were reminders of the old life of the city: ornate warehouses built in the style of earlier trading empires, Byzantine from the Mediterranean or Moghul from India. The international flavour comes across with great force. Quite near the canal I noticed a commercial building topped with an ornate cupola, and on that cupola was a weather vane in the shape of an old trading ship from the days of sail. The canal itself occupies the narrowest of narrow corridors. No room here for luxuries such as overspill weirs. In wet weather, the water simply pours straight over the tops of the locks, so that an adventurous canoeist could travel the entire length of the canal through Manchester without pausing once. There is not even space for a towpath along much of the route, which at least brought me up to

A subterranean approach to the centre of Manchester as the canal disappears among the concrete columns that form the foundations of a modern office block.

street level for a closer look at this old commercial quarter. The boaters on the canal see little beyond the high, enclosing walls.

It all came to an end at Chesterfield junction, which is also in a way a beginning. For here, the Rochdale meets the old Bridgewater Canal, the first waterway to reach the heart of Manchester, the canal that brought the whole canal age to life. Yet within a matter of metres, you also find the Manchester Ship Canal, the very last attempt to bring commercial water-borne traffic to the city. The old life, the busy, thrusting life of ships and barges is over now, but the city itself grew on the basis of these simple beginnings. The Duke of Bridgewater's Canal and others helped Manchester to grow as surely as did the cotton trade they served. As I walked on up into the city streets, it all seemed a very long way from the weavers' cottages up in the Pennines. So it is, but it seemed appropriate to end here in the middle of a modern city. It is all too easy to see the modern world as some self-sufficient entity, rather than as simply the latest stage in a continuing story that stretches back through the centuries.

I started these walks on an ancient trackway and, no doubt, early man walked through Manchester Piccadilly at a time when even a simple village was a concept that still lay in the future. This last walk has, I hope, shown that town and country are not only joined physically by the threads of transport, but historically as well. The industries the canals were built to serve first drew their power from the rushing hill streams. They grew up in an age when the worker was as likely to be found in a stone-built cottage on the moors as in a terrace crowded among a multitude of others in a city centre. This walk, like all the others, had shown me change – and had shown change as a continuous process stretching far back into the past and onwards into an inconceivable future. Yet, just as the time slice of each walk has represented only a small fraction of the whole, so each walk has only been one among an infinite number that could be taken. On every walk I was struck by the vast number of clues to the historical past, and I have no doubt at all that I missed far more clues than I spotted. If I set off along the Rochdale again tomorrow I might well view it in a very different light. And that surely is the great appeal of walking with, as it were, one's historical eyes open: you never stop learning. And I have never lost that special thrill that comes with discovery, that feeling that you have stumbled across some reminder of the ancient past, and all you have to do is use your eyes and your brain for the rest of the story to be revealed. Any readers who decide to follow my footsteps will not just be seeing what I saw, but finding new clues of their own: I just hope they find as much pleasure and enjoyment as I did along the way.

FURTHER READING

Aston, Michael and Bond, James. 1976. *The Landscape of Towns.* Dent, London.

Brown, R Allen. 1976. *English Castles.* Batsford, London.

Brunskill, R W. 1971. *Illustrated Handbook of Vernacular Architecture.* Faber.

Burton, Anthony. 1983. *The National Trust uide to Our Industrial Past.* George Philip.

Burton, Anthony and May, John. 1986. *Landscape Detective.* Unwin Hyman.

Clayton, Peter. 1985. *Archaeological Sites of Great Britain.* Batsford.

Clifton-Taylor, Alec. 1972. *The Pattern of English Building.* Faber.

Hoskins, W G. 1977. *The Making of the English Landscape.* Hodder and Stoughton.

Hoskins W G (ed.). *The Making of the English Landscape* series (separate volumes cover individual counties). Hodder and Stoughton.

Hunter, Tom. 1984. *West Highland Way.* Constable.

Jebb, Miles. 1984. *A Guide to the South Downs Way.* Constable.

Margary, Ivan D. 1955. *Roman Roads in Britain,* (2 vols). Phoenix House.

Morgan, Kenneth O (ed.). 1984. *The Oxford Illustrated History of Britain.* Oxford University Press.

Muir, Richard. 1981. *Shell Guide to Reading the Landscape.* Michael Joseph.

Ordnance Survey. 1973. *Field Archaeology in Great Britain.* HMSO.

Rackham, Oliver. 1976. *Trees and Woodland in the British Landscape.* Dent.

Renfrew, Colin (ed.). 1985. *The Prehistory of Orkney.* Edinburgh University Press.

Rowley, Trevor. 1978. *Villages in the Landscape.* Dent.

Taylor, Christopher. 1975. *Fields in the Landscape.* Dent.

Taylor, Christopher. 1979. *Roads and Tracks of Britain.* Dent.

Trueman, A.E. 1963. *Geology and Scenery in England and Wales.* Penguin.

ACKNOWLEDGEMENTS

All photographs by the author with the exception of: page 59, The Cambridge University Collection of Air Photographs; page 80, Crown Copyright, Historic Buildings and Monuments, Scotland.

INDEX

Numbers in *italics* refer to illustrations.